A Textured Life:
Empowerment
and
Adults with Developmental Disabilities

Alison Pedlar, Larry Haworth, Peggy Hutchison,
Andrew Taylor, and Peter Dunn

Wilfrid Laurier University Press

This book has been published with the help of a grant from the Humanities and Social Sciences Federation of Canada, using funds provided by the Social Sciences and Humanities Research Council of Canada.

We acknowledge the financial support of the Government of Canada through the Book Publishing Industry Development Program for our publishing activities.

Canadian Cataloguing in Publication Data

A textured life : empowerment and adults with developmental disabilities

Includes bibliographical references and index.
ISBN 0-88920-335-0

1. Developmentally disabled – Canada.   2. Developmentally disabled – Services for – Canada.   I. Pedlar, Alison, 1945-   .

HV1570.5.C3T49 1999   361.1'968'00971   C99-930401-1

© 1999
Wilfrid Laurier University Press
Waterloo, Ontario, Canada N2L 3C5

Cover design by Leslie Macredie, using a detail from *The Sun's Garden* by Stephanie Kirkwood Walker.

Printed in Canada

A Textured Life: Empowerment and Adults with Developmental Disabilities has been produced from a manuscript supplied in camera-ready form by the author.

For the women and men who contributed their stories to this book

CONTENTS

ACKNOWLEDGEMENTS

This book has been made possible through the extraordinary generosity of members of communities across Canada. Over the course of many months, we met and talked with individuals with developmental disabilities, many family members, and support people. In these personal exchanges, people essentially invited us into their lives. They gave enormous amounts of time—reflecting, reviewing, and responding to our many questions about their experiences with community life in Canada. We took so much from them, it is our hope that this book will allow us to give something back.

Lots of people helped with the work that culminated in this book. In appreciation of the considerable contribution that each one made, we want to mention their names here—Annemarie Schweitzer for her careful work in helping us get the survey out that started the whole process; Louis and Marie-Andrée Groarke with translation, and Marie-Andrée for interviewing our francophone participants; Susan Tirone for interviewing and data gathering; Christine Vanditelli for assisting in site visits and data recording; Elizabeth van Dreunen for many hours of transcribing interview tapes; Sandy DeVisser similarly; and Margaret Schneider for her care and attention to the editing and formatting of the final manuscript. The principal research assistant in the project was Susan Arai, whose exceptional commitment and skill in data analysis helped us bring the project to completion.

The project was made possible with a grant from the Social Sciences and Humanities Research Council of Canada. Additional funding was provided by the Scottish Rite Foundation and the University of Waterloo.

PREFACE

Most adults with developmental disabilities live in a very different world than was the case three decades ago. Then, life in large institutions was the norm. Deinstitutionalization was heralded as bringing about a "return to the community." Now, over 30 years later, new social policies have been adopted to support adults with developmental disabilities in our communities. In many ways these individuals, those who were released from large institutions to return to the community and those who have never experienced life in a large institution, are confronted with a new reality. We will be discussing some aspects of this new reality, focussing on how it is being experienced by adults with developmental disabilities themselves. The features of their experiences that especially interest us are suggested by the terms "empowerment" and "community": In what ways do they find the new reality empowering? In what ways do they find that they are accepted as members of the community with valued roles to play?

This is the account of a cross-Canada study we conducted to answer these and other similar questions. From the outset, we realized that in order to more fully understand community life and empowerment, as experienced by adults with developmental disabilities, we would need to examine two fundamental issues. First, we would need to determine the approaches to support that were in place in Canada. Second, we would need to examine the impact of these approaches as experienced by adults with developmental disabilities themselves. Thus, the study fell naturally into two phases. The first phase involved a cross-Canada survey of service providers; that is, agencies providing support services to adults with developmental disabilities, to determine what services exist in Canada. The second phase would then take us to several different regions of the country for face-to-face interviews with adults with developmental disabilities to explore with them the impact of these approaches on their day-to-day life.

The Survey

In the first phase, the cross-Canada survey was sent to all agencies we were able to identify by two principal sources: provincial government ministries responsible for services to adults with developmental disabilities, and provincial Associations for Community Living. As suggested by the issues that were of concern to us, the primary purpose of the survey was to establish a detailed picture of the service landscape as it affects adults with developmental disabilities. The survey asked questions regarding the service provider's mandate, the number of people served, the range of services provided, funding procedures, planning of services and supports, whether families were involved in the lives of the individuals served, and whether the agency had participation from community members, family members, and persons with disabilities on their boards and committees. Questionnaires were delivered to 1336 service providers, of whom 801 responded, for a response rate of 60%.

This survey was among the most comprehensive of its kind in Canada, but it cannot be regarded as a total accounting of the services to adults with developmental disabilities in the country. In 1996, the Roeher Institute, which is the research arm of the Canadian Association of Community Living, produced data related to residential service providers in Canada that serve four or more people in any one residence. As they pointed out, it is extremely difficult to ascertain the full extent and range of services in Canada. We reached the vast majority of service providers that received provincial government funds. As well, we knew that we were reaching the bulk of the Association for Community Living service provider member organizations across the country. However, there were likely some groups, funded from other sources and not part of the Association for Community Living, that were not included in the study. Nevertheless, the survey captured a broad cross-section of services and provided information on the numbers of people supported, the types of support, and the manner in which these supports were planned, funded, and delivered.

The Qualitative Interviews

In the second phase we selected ten service providers or agencies in five different regions of Canada which had participated in the survey. Our objective was to select agencies that offered a wide range of approaches, so that altogether they would provide a solid basis for understanding the sorts of services, service philosophies, and funding arrangements found across Canada. At these agencies we met with 141 individuals—52 adults with developmental disabilities, 26 family members, and 63 staff and other support providers—to learn how they, especially the individuals with developmental disabilities, were experiencing the reality that the new policies had created. As suggested above, we were interested in two large values, empowerment and community: In what ways do adults with developmental disabilities flourish in the new reality and find life in the community to be empowering? And to what extent and in what ways do they feel that they really belong to the community? But these ideas are too large and grand to employ directly. More particularly, then, we asked: How do adults with developmental disabilities experience their new living arrangements, their family life, life in the workplace, their leisure? And what sort of relationships with others do they have? With this information in hand, we wanted to explore the connections between these experiences and the approaches to social support that were in place, including funding arrangements. We are very grateful to these individuals for sharing their experiences with us.

In the pages that follow, after two introductory chapters (chapters 1 and 2), we report on what people told us, often using their own words (chapters 3-5), and then, having in mind these words, we tentatively draw some conclusions from what we learned (chapters 6 and 7). The conclusions are both theoretical and practical. Our conversations with adults who are developmentally disabled and those in their circles of support have led us to the view that when the new social support policies have worked, from the perspective of developmentally disabled adults themselves, it is because the policies have led to changes that have enabled these adults to enjoy *textured lives*. This means that their life experiences are not defined only by their disability, but they interact meaningfully with a variety of people and are engaged in a number of diverse activities, with the result that their lives transcend the "world of disability." It scarcely needs mentioning that, however extensive the services they provided may have been, large institutions confined their residents to just this world of disability.

Thinking about the role of texture in people's lives has led us to a *social ecological theory* of empowerment and community. This, along with the idea of textured lives, is spelled out in greater detail in chapter 6. We shall only say here that the social ecological theory centres on the importance of context and supportive relationships. It advances the claim that empowerment is not a zero-sum game by which one person may be empowered only at the expense of another person's disempowerment. Rather, the supportive relationships that empower one of the persons in the relationship, by that very fact may empower the others as well, so that they all flourish together.

Chapter 1

CITIZENSHIP AND COMMUNITY LIFE

Well, my buddy, he's going to a workshop like this, they call it CP workshop, you know what it sounds like. I started there, then I got hauled in the office and they said to me, "We've got a better job for you; don't think we are trying to get rid of you, we are trying to get you in a better position." If I ever knew what I know now, I would have never started there. This was 30 years ago, not now. I started in school, I was getting trained. I made a couple of end tables, I made a couple of legs for tables. I was just starting to make salad bowls. From there I went to CP workshop, from there I went to Crippled Civilians. (Howard, employee in workshop)

The Beginnings of an Understanding

In this study we have attempted to understand empowerment and community from the perspective of people who've been labelled developmentally disabled. Howard, the man who speaks in this opening comment about his friend at a "CP [cerebral palsy] workshop," is one of the adults who met with us during this study. He talked about his life and helped us gain an understanding of life in the community as experienced by adults with developmental disabilities. Howard's reflections give us a glimpse of the challenges that the people we met with have to deal with on a daily basis. Whether one is talking about where people live, what sorts of work they do, or the control they have over basic life choices, the hurdles that adults who are labelled developmentally disabled have to overcome continue to present extraordinary challenges.

Our intent in gathering information from people on their experiences of community living was to gain an understanding of how different ways of providing support to adults with developmental disabilities affected their daily lives. We wanted to learn what the adults themselves felt about formal support services and their informal support systems. We wanted to understand how the adults themselves felt about different approaches to the provision of social support. We wanted to hear stories about how different kinds of formal and informal support had helped or hindered their process of personal empowerment and the extent of their engagement in the wider community. We felt the best way of doing this was to meet and talk with them personally. We

1

also knew that there would be people around these individuals that we should speak with as well, including family members and paid staff, to gain as much insight as possible into the experience of social support as it exists in Canada today. In the pages that follow, we have included many of the insights and observations that came from the people we met. Based on these insights and the discussion of people's experiences, we also sought to understand why it is that some approaches to support are more empowering than others and are generally felt to enhance people's quality of life and their participation in the life of the community. *Ultimately, our goal was to develop a theory of empowerment that incorporates both personal and social dimensions, so that it is also a theory of community.*

Support of persons with disabilities has changed over the last several decades. Services were once centred in institutions. As the rights of persons with disabilities began to enter the public dialogue in the 1960s, it became clear that societies ought never again to place people who had been labelled into large, segregated living arrangements. Institutions as they existed through the first half of this century would no longer be tolerated. So began the long and sometimes difficult process of closing institutions and developing community living arrangements. It was envisaged, even if not spoken of in terms of empowerment, that deinstitutionalization would allow people to have choices, live more normal lives, and become active participants in community life, in contrast to the disempowering situations that existed for people in institutions.

For over twenty years now, deinstitutionalization has been studied by researchers from all over the world and from numerous disciplines. There is agreement that community living affirms individual rights and gives people with disabilities the chance to live, work, and recreate *alongside* other citizens. More recently, however, we have begun to recognize the enormous divergence in what community living actually means in terms of people's well-being (O'Brien & O'Brien, 1991). Important questions arise: Are the group homes and other living arrangements that have replaced large institution dorm life anything more than mini-institutions? As adults with developmental disabilities move around in the community to which many of them have been "returned," do they feel that they are genuinely part of the community, that they belong? Do they enjoy meaningful relationships with other citizens, not just people with developmental disabilities? Or is their world still largely defined by their disability?

It is evident that formal social support policies—that is, those many policies that cover everything from disability pensions, to schooling, to paid work—determine much of the experience of community living and people's ability to take control of their own lives (Peck, 1991). Social support as we are using it here refers to ways and means that are in place within a society to ensure people have access to resources that respond to their basic needs. In the last two decades, our understanding of this social and cultural process has evolved significantly. We now see the limitations of an approach that commodifies social support—views it as a simple transaction in which one person provides another with resources he or she needs. We have come to understand that the sharing of support is a profoundly social process that inheres in the ways people interact with one another day-to-day and communicate their acceptance. Botschner (1996) argues that social support is not about what people get from one another, or even about what they perceive themselves as getting. Support is about interpersonal interactions that help the interacting parties to sustain or restore a sense of shared meaning.

Social support influences every aspect of a person's day-to-day life. Social policy and social service provision are expressions of a society's commitment to assist vulnerable citizens. Social support, therefore, will influence what sort of lives people with developmental disabilities lead: where and with whom they live, the sort of work they do, whether they get competitive wages for their work, what sort of control they have over their disposable income. As well, social support is evident in the human relationships that are present within (and to a large extent constitute) a community, and so of interest are friendships, whether adults with disabilities consider their staff to be their friends, and whether their friends include both people with and without disabilities. What do they do that takes them outside of the human service sector; that is, beyond contact with paid staff and others served by paid staff? What sorts of things do people do outside of the work day and do they get to take vacations away from their usual place of residence? What sorts of opportunities do people have for involvement with the community at large, including making a contribution?

Sensitive to these issues and concerns, we set out to look at the structure of human service systems, including funding mechanisms, which were specifically directed toward supporting adults with developmental disabilities in Canada. We were interested in questions of self-determination, empowerment, and community, and whether the service system operated in a manner which allowed people to move beyond states of dependency. In the past decade we have seen the emergence of new approaches to support. New funding mechanisms, by which people receive individualized funding, were occasionally available. As well, reorganization of services produced less formal groupings of support people, so that individuals had clusters of people around them, involving some paid and some unpaid people. However, relatively little was known about the ways in which the support systems that were in place enhanced or hindered the quality of people's community life experiences.

A Point of View

Researchers always have a point of view that in various ways influences the research they do. The present study is no exception. It is important that we state at the beginning what the values are that we bring to this study of support services for adults with developmental disabilities.

We believe that two broad values should guide support services, and, indeed, social services policy in general. We feel that the indicators of success for social services policy are the impact policy has on the *empowerment of everyone affected by it,* and its tendency to *bring these people together into relations of community.* In fact, we see the two halves of this vision as indivisible, and believe that there is but one overarching value: empowerment-in-community.

Many other researchers who study support services for adults with developmental disabilities share this commitment to the values of empowerment and community. Concern that people be empowered in the community underlay much of the deinstitutionalization movement and probably contributed to the motivation to actually close the large institutions. More recently, criticism of group homes as small-scale institutions often seems prompted by the same values. Social role valorization theory, normalization theory, the independent living movement, inclusion and self-advocacy theories, the developmental paradigm, and the quality of life model—all of these perspectives appear to rest on a commitment to either empowerment or community or both. When a theory (or perspective) focusses on the rights of people with disabilities, the value placed uppermost is empowerment or autonomy. This is because the very idea of a right singles out the individual as of prime importance and consists in asserting a claim against the community. Normalization theory, by contrast, focusses on the community. By normalizing the environment of a person with disabilities, we ensure that it is the same as or at least resembles the environment of those who aren't disabled. Of course, one can agree with these observations without supposing that those who focus primarily on rights must reject the idea of community, or that those who focus primarily on normalizing the environment must deny that people have rights.

What perhaps does differentiate our commitment to the values of empowerment and community from that of many other researchers in the field of social services for adults with developmental disabilities is our view that the two values go hand in hand. We believe that neither is finally achievable without the other, so that policy that pursues one must be equally sensitive to the need to achieve the other. As we shall see, this close relationship between empowerment and community is especially important for persons with developmental disabilities. Because such persons are more vulnerable than the population at large, policies that focus on enhancing empowerment at the expense of community—for example, by privatizing domains that previously had existed as public goods, and thus making them less accessible to those with limited financial resources—are likely to leave people with developmental disabilities worse off.

Empowerment and community are buzzwords. Like all buzzwords, they are used in different ways by different people and are often vague or ambiguous. In order to clarify where we are coming from here, it is important that we give as much precision to these words as we can. It is not important to offer formal definitions. Instead, we want to call attention to some aspects of empowerment and community that we regard as important and to correct what we believe to be some misapprehensions.

Empowerment

In our view, empowerment, freedom, and autonomy all refer to roughly the same condition. Sometimes a distinction is made between autonomy and empowerment, so that empowerment refers to the process of gaining autonomy. For example, we think of someone who is in control of their life as being autonomous, and we think of a change that enhances their control over their life as empowering them. As one connects the two, the important idea is that of a person being in control of his or her life. Unfortunately, this notion of being in control of one's life is often understood very narrowly.

For example, often empowerment, autonomy, and freedom are reduced to the idea of having choices. There may be some basis for reducing the idea of freedom to that of choice. But it seems evident to us that, although having choices is important, it does not guarantee empowerment and autonomy. If empowerment meant nothing more than choice, then closure of large institutions and return of the "inmates," as they were once called, to the community would be an unalloyed gain. No thought would need to be given to meeting the needs of people with developmental disabilities in the community, since once the large institution's restraints are removed "everything is permitted." But this alone is not empowering: Where everything is permitted it may be that nothing is possible.

A richer understanding of empowerment can be arrived at by thinking about the underlying idea of people being in control of their lives. Residents of group homes have some latitude in planning their meal menus and in organizing their leisure time. In these areas they are at least likely to have considerably greater freedom of choice than was available in large institutions. Instead of just being presented with their evening meal and finding their leisure activities programmed by a person whose job it is to arrange such matters, they may actually have to decide whether, where, and what to eat, and how to fill their spare hours. But do these choices in and of themselves put people in control of their lives when lack of financial resources drastically restricts what they may actually buy? When many of the leisure facilities they would enjoy using are inaccessible or inhospitable to them? When they lack information regarding their real options? Or when lack of experience and confidence serve to reduce real options to unrealizable dreams?

When the issue is how much a person is in control of his or her own life, considerations such as these get to the heart of the matter. As we shall see, the narratives of the people who participated in this exploration with us exhibit time and time again how the real constraints they experience do not arise from being denied by legal and institutional rules the opportunity to make choices. More or less everything *is* permitted. Nevertheless, they are constrained by lack of accessibility and availability of resources, including information, and, more subtly, by such matters as lacking self-confidence and not having supportive relationships that provide the background of security and trust from which one may find the strength to venture out into uncharted waters.

In our view, then, empowerment has two dimensions that go beyond choice. First there is an internal dimension that refers to an empowered person's own resources. This includes people being able to realize their goals, to know what options they have, and to decide whether taking up an option is, all things considered, the course they want to follow (Haworth, 1986). It includes motivational factors, such as a willingness to take risks and to persist in the face of obstacles and setbacks. It includes the ability to relate with others to enlist their help when this is needed. For obvious reasons, it includes self-confidence and self-esteem. And it includes the ability to follow through on choices that have been made by actually taking the steps that the decided-upon course of action requires.

In thinking of the extent to which a person is empowered with respect to this internal dimension, we ask whether the person lives in a setting and has access to a circle of support that reinforces his or her strengths by providing encouragement, instruction where needed, reassurance, trust, and unconditional love and caring. In our view, empowerment in this personal dimension is not a mere matter of the inventory of personal assets with which people begin. It is more a matter of what people are able to do with the assets they have and of how well their circles of support enable them to flourish.

But a person's empowerment does not depend entirely on personal qualities. It is also affected by social or external realities. Here, too, being empowered involves much more than simply having choices. It is obvious that to be empowered people require a nurturing environment. In part, this is touched on in the reference to circles of support in the preceding paragraph. There, the idea was the ways supportive people can bring out one's personal strengths. But beyond this, it matters whether people's environment contains the necessary means for taking up the options available to them. Everything we do, except possibly daydreaming, is done with the aid of tangible and often intangible tools and resources. People need at least pencil and paper to write, reliable information to think clearly, transportation to go shopping. Insofar as we lack the means for doing the things we want to do, or the ability to acquire these means, we enjoy less control over our life. Without these resources, many of the everyday activities that form a normal life cannot be done, or can be done only with great difficulty. Anyone who lacks these resources—food, a job, transportation, friends, a lover, a comfortable home—is to that extent disempowered.

The social dimension of empowerment also has a structural aspect. A normal round of life splits into a number of spheres that enshrine different practices. Thus, we move, for instance, from the sphere of family life to those of work, religious worship, leisure activity, education, and so on. The practices we engage in while inhabiting these spheres confront us as somewhat fixed structures. Having a job involves having a job description. Although there is bound to be some scope for choice, to some extent we do what the job requires or don't keep the job (Haworth, 1986).

This structural aspect is fateful for anyone's empowerment. The various spheres into which a normal round of life splits may be liberating or constraining. They may lead us to a life that releases our energies; alternatively, the sphere may be deadening and depressing. In our view, a practical commitment to empowerment as a value must involve paying close attention to the details of the practices that make up a normal round of life and to the ways these practices might be altered so that they become more liberating than constraining, more enlivening than deadening.

Up to a point then, the issue of empowerment for people with developmental disabilities is the same as the issue of empowerment for everyone. This is because there is a common set of practices that confront all alike and give shape to all of our lives. We all walk the same streets, shop the same stores, go off to the same or at least similar workplaces. So far as this is true, we may say that the empowerment of people with developmental disabilities cannot be enhanced unless the common set of practices is better adapted to human needs, becomes less constraining and more liberating. The empowerment of any member of the society waits on the empowerment of all members.

But of course this is only a part of the truth. What is more important is that the common practices are accessed differently by different groups; in particular, adults with developmental disabilities have special needs with respect to the common practices. We do not want to lose sight of the fact that, to a large extent, empowerment for those who are developmentally disabled requires policy changes that would affect the practices that give shape to everyone's life and impact the empowerment of all. But here we are especially interested to understand the ways adults with developmental disabilities experience these practices—how they are found to be working with respect to empowerment, and how they are found to be failing—so that meaningful adaptations may be made.

Community

The second idea that needs preliminary clarification is that of community. Loss of community has been a familiar theme in Western literature for over 150 years. Naturally, since the theme is one of something lost, this literature is nostalgic. It idealizes an earlier time when people were closer to one another and lives were more focussed on and dedicated to the groups into which people were formed, especially in villages and small towns. Because it is a nostalgia for the communal relations that are imagined to have prevailed in these villages and small towns, the theme idealizes spatially based community. The communal relations that existed then are invidiously contrasted with the self-interestedness, anonymity, privatization, and narcissism of contemporary life.

In our opinion, though, the ideal of community is not and should not be mere nostalgia for an earlier time. Nor need community be spatially based. Community, we believe, is not just a matter of geography but also of relationships, of the quality of relationships. People have community with one another when they are brought together in a common concern or cause, or even in a common practice to which they attach value. As well, when people who are engaged together in a practice form a community, they are not just trying get something out of it for themselves. Two people haggling over the price of a thing that one wants to sell and the other wants to buy do not form a community. Unless, that is, both regard haggling over prices as part of a way of life that should be kept up, rather than just a way to get a good deal. It is this dependence of community on shared values and concerns and on mutually valued ways of life that makes self-interestedness, anonymity, privatization, and narcissism the counterforces to community (Haworth, 1977).

Our earlier remark, that empowering people with developmental disabilities cannot be disassociated from the empowering of people generally, seems to apply to community as well. Unless there is community in the society at large, people with developmental disabilities will not find community: Although we speak of the "return to the community," there would be no community to return to, only a place where people pursue their own private lives and concerns.

Community and openness. For adults with developmental disabilities, however, the problem is not so much that modern life seems to be marked by loss of community as that the communities that exist are often closed to them, at least to some extent. At the extreme we have gated communities and privatized facilities that are open only to those who can pay the price of admission. "Not in my backyard" attitudes often keep neighbourhoods effectively closed without resort to actual gates. People whom society has marginalized, as well as those with special needs, are often excluded as a result. And if the present aura that surrounds the idea of privatization persists, such people may find themselves further excluded by a proliferation of closed communities. For adults with developmental disabilities to really belong to the community, openness must become the order of the day. In saying this, we aren't objecting to privatization as such, but only to its spread to the point where no or few public goods remain and people who lack the means of acquiring private goods are reduced to a miserable, marginalized existence.

Empowerment vs. community. The opposition between the idea of community, on one hand, and, on the other, the family of ideas to which empowerment and autonomy belong, including freedom, rights and liberty, goes back 300 years to the onset of the Enlightenment. Liberalism in the original sense—the political philosophy of John Locke, Immanuel Kant, and John Stuart Mill—took its stand on liberty, freedom, rights, and autonomy and was suspicious of the claims of community. Burkean conservatives, the German romantics, and Hegel, took their stand on community and sought to minimize the importance of freedom and of the individual, and his or her rights. This historical opposition of the ideas of freedom and community is played out in the now prevalent view that empowerment and community are opposed.

Empowerment-in-Community

Whatever the merits of the historical debate, between the original liberals and Burkean conservatives for example, our own belief is that empowerment and community are mutually reinforcing, so that there is no need to make a choice between the two. To express this connection, we speak of "empowerment-in-community." This formula points to a number of related ideas. For example, we believe that to be valuable, a community must be made up of empowered persons. Who would want to live in a closely knit community of robots or of people who never think for themselves? As well, unless they live or could live in relations of community with others, empowered persons could well be a threat to us all. We doubt that the ideal of empowerment is worth pursuing, or we regard its importance to be seriously diminished, if the empowered persons are to end up living self-interested, anonymous, narcissistic, or privatized lives. Rather, it is especially when empowered people live in, or are ready to live in, relations of community with others that their state of empowerment warrants our admiration. And it is especially when such conditions prevail that the goal of enhancing people's empowerment is worth pursuing.

In effect, we are announcing our commitment to two ideas: empowering the members of a community enhances the value of the community, and helping a group of empowered persons to come together as a community enhances the value of their empowerment. We also hold the closely related belief that empowerment and community go together in actual fact. That is, if we want to enhance the quality of community in our lives we will need to empower ourselves as well; and, from the other side, we will have little success empowering ourselves if we neglect the quality of community in our lives. This is to say, then, that empowerment and community are mutually enhancing and mutually supportive.

It should be easy to see the relevance of these abstract observations concerning the relations between community and empowerment for a study of social support policies for adults with developmental disabilities. If empowerment and community are mutually supportive and mutually enhancing, as is expressed by the formula "empowerment-in-community," then social support for adults with developmental disabilities needs to go beyond provision of group homes, workshops, and special transportation services that deliver these individuals in a block to leisure facilities in the community. Such arrangements and facilities provide ways of filling the time and keeping people busy, but they are not especially empowering; although they bring adults with developmental disabilities out into the community, they do not advance the interest these individuals have in achieving a greater sense of belonging to the community and of participating in the life of the community in interaction with the mainstream population.

Our approach here is "inductive" in that we do not want to impose a normative point of view on the study from the beginning. We don't assume that our values, however continuous they may be with the mainstream of Western thought since the Enlightenment, fit the life experiences of adults with developmental disabilities. Clearly, it would be better to let substantive conclusions grow out of conversations with adults with developmental disabilities themselves and those in their circles of support. Accordingly, in the context of this study, "empowerment-in-community" has the status of a leading idea that sensitized us to values implicit in the experiences of the individuals with whom we spoke.

A Social Ecological Theory

As remarked in the preface and explained at greater length in chapter 7, this study supports a social ecological view of empowerment. It is a familiar thought that in natural ecosystems living things must find in their habitat the conditions for their flourishing. When the habitat lacks nutrients and other conditions essential for the inhabitants' growth, then of course the inhabitants become stunted and eventually die off. But also typically in such ecosystems a balance is achieved. Each colony of living things finds in the habitat the conditions for its flourishing, and in turn by flourishing maintains the habitat in a state that promotes the flourishing of the other colonies. Thus, trees and vines in the rain forest find nutrients that promote luxuriant growth, and by forming a canopy above the forest floor create the moist environment that sustains other colonies of living things; these living things, in turn, by growing over the forest floor, ensure an abundant supply of the nutrients on which the trees and vines depend. In natural ecosystems, relationships are symbiotic.

The social ecological theory finds that much the same holds in human relationships. The narratives reported in the following chapters strongly support the sensitizing ideas of empowerment and community as these have been interpreted above. These narratives suggest that those who contribute to the empowerment of adults with developmental disabilities do so by entering into relationships that are empowering for them as well. Thus, adults with developmental disabilities and those in their circles of support discover empowerment-in-community. That is, when their habitat is empowering, then often their relationships with one another are symbiotic and they form a community. Of course, this is a happy outcome and is not always guaranteed. But it is a hopeful conclusion because it lays to rest the thought that the mainstream society will suffer, financially and otherwise, if it adopts policies for adults with developmental disabilities that truly empower them and give to them a sense of belonging in and to the community.

The feature of the social ecological theory that is most relevant in this connection is its stress on the importance of *texture* in people's lives. The term is a metaphor but we believe that it fairly aptly describes the situation of adults with developmental disabilities who have actually achieved empowerment-in-community. The significant contrast is with life in a large institution, which is grey and unidimensional. There the residents' world is largely defined by their disability. When adults with developmental disabilities find that they are not just physically present in the larger community but actually have a *life* there which brings them into meaningful relationships with a wide range of others, when they find that the community offers and encourages participation in mainstream community affairs, then their lives gain depth and colour. From the community's side, the outstanding prerequisite is *openness*—not just the formal openness that occurs when no one confronts legal barriers to participation, but openness that entails being welcomed in, encouraged, and actually supported. For adults with developmental disabilities, the result is a textured life. They are empowered by meaningfully connecting themselves with the community. The abstraction, empowerment-in-community, is made concrete in textured lives.

Chapter 2

THE SUPPORT SERVICES LANDSCAPE

Social change can travel in two opposite directions. A move in one direction—the progressive road—moves us towards social justice and a fairer sharing of resources and power. The other direction—the oppressive road—takes us to a country based on greater privilege, greater inequality, and an increasing concentration of power in fewer hands. (Carniol, 1995, p.113)

Introduction

Studies and commentaries on Canadian social policy and human service systems have pointed to ways in which existing legislation and policies tend to disempower rather than empower individuals who receive social support (Armitage, 1996; Djao, 1983; Guest, 1985; Jongbloed & Crichton, 1990; Lord & Hutchison, 1996; McGilly, 1991; Moscovitch & Albert, 1987; Pedlar, 1991; Wharf, 1992). It is not unusual for people who receive social assistance to feel a sense of inadequacy. People who are unable to find employment in the labour market often become less and less able to imagine a life in which they are in control of day-to-day decisions and events. People with disabilities are no exception. When people's lives are shaped by external forces to such an extent that they have no sense of a future, something must be wrong with the system. When these problems persist for as long as they have, despite major structural changes to the service delivery system, one must begin to identify fundamental assumptions that have remained unchallenged.

Rioux and Richler (1995) have argued that the life stories of people with developmental disabilities are powerful test cases for anyone interested in identifying and understanding the ways in which our system continues to foster dependency. People living with this label have struggled for a voice even within the disability rights movement. They often face complex combinations of physical, psychological, economic, and social barriers. They are amongst the most devalued and disempowered people in our society. Commenting on the shift in perspective that accompanied the 1992 change in the American definition of developmental disabilities, where the system of support takes precedence over the diagnosis, Luckasson & Spitalnik (1994) note that:

With this change has come the end of the readiness model, in which people with mental retardation earned their right to community membership, and the beginning of an emphasis on self-determination and empowerment. The images of dependence have been transformed to calls for self-definition, personal autonomy, and choice. (p. 84)

As has often been observed, one of the hallmarks of a service system based on the "readiness model" is that it strives to divide those who are ready or worthy from those who are not, emphasizing diagnosis. In contrast, a system based on upholding the equal rights of all citizens includes and respects everyone, most notably those who are marginalized and require particular support. This is one of the reasons why we feel a book like this one—a book that examines how successful our society has been at creating services and policies that support self-determination and empowerment for people labelled as developmentally disabled—is important. It has been partly through the emergence of a body of literature related to community-building (Carling, 1995; McKnight, 1995; O'Connell, 1988; Trainor, Pomeroy, & Pape, 1993) and empowerment of individuals and families (Borthwick-Duffy, 1996; Centre for Research and Education in Human Services, 1988; Dunst, Trivette, & Lapointe, 1992; Gottlieb, 1985; 1998; Jones, Garlow, Turnbull III, & Barber, 1996), that the need for change in the funding and structure of human services specifically designed for people with developmental disabilities has been brought to the public's attention (Roeher Institute, 1991; 1993a).

The structure of the support system, including funding approaches, has implications for the opportunities for self-definition, personal autonomy, individual choice, and inclusion in community life about which Luckasson and Spitalnik are talking. Traditionally, policies and support systems intended to enable people with developmental disabilities to live in community settings have funded programs or services rather than individuals. The most familiar of these models of support involves the transfer of government funds to "transfer agencies." These agencies are charged with the responsibility of administering programs and providing support services to people in their care. The results of our survey (detailed in appendix I), indicate that the service landscape continues to be based principally in transfer agencies which provide a wide range of programs, many of which take place in segregated settings specifically for this population. Under this frequently adopted model, decisions regarding the needs and services of the individual are made by professionals and by agency personnel and agency board members who represent community interests. The transfer agency is generally seen as accountable to the funder rather than to individuals and families. People rarely leave the service of the transfer agency and there is a natural concern that this model of support essentially perpetuates dependency.

Some have proposed individualized funding as a more innovative and responsive alternative to the traditional funding of programs delivered by transfer agencies. "Individualized funding" refers to funds which go directly from the government to the individual, ostensibly affording the individual more choice and control over the support services required to meet his or her daily needs. Proponents of this approach to support suggest that it is more likely to lead to empowerment of people with disabilities, allowing individuals to break through the state of dependency which has characterized the more traditional models of support (Agosta, 1989; Lord, 1991; Roeher Institute, 1991; 1993a; 1993b, 1993c; Salisbury, Dickey, & Crawford, 1987).

Our study provided an opportunity to examine support services to adults with developmental disabilities in Canada, including the range of funding approaches that are utilized in various parts of the country. As well, the philosophical value base that underlies service provision and the delivery of supports is often indicative of the sorts of lives people are able to live, and of whether or not they are likely to be in a position to move beyond the "images of dependence." This was something else that we were interested in knowing more about and so we included in the study an examination of the philosophies, as expressed in mission statements, that characterize services, particularly in conjunction with any newer funding approaches that we were able to identify in agencies across Canada.

Pursuing these interests, we identified the *funding arrangements* which appeared most prevalent in Canada, and took a look at whether there was evidence to suggest that traditional funding approaches were being replaced by other, more individualized alternatives such as direct individualized funding. We also identified the dominant *organizational values and philosophies* in the service landscape, and asked whether these funding arrangements and organizational philosophies varied by agency type, i.e., between the non-profit services that have traditionally dominated this sector and the emerging for-profit agencies which reflect more of a business orientation. They did, and we'll discuss these momentarily.

Philosophies That Have Guided Services Historically

In order to place our observations in context, we feel it is important to provide some historical background to the evolution of the major service philosophies that have played a key role in shaping support services to persons with developmental disabilities in Canada over the past forty years. Much of the current service structure for persons with developmental disabilities can be traced back to the efforts of parents in the 1950s and early 1960s. These pioneers went against the conventional wisdom of the day and decided not to place their daughters and sons in institutions. The parent movement that evolved from these beginnings was first known as the Canadian Association for the Mentally Retarded (CAMR), which is the forerunner to what today in Canada is called the Canadian Association for Community Living (CACL). CACL and its local units, Associations for Community Living (ACLs), were among the primary advocacy groups to lobby for community-based services and to speak out about the welfare of people still living in institutions. In what came to be called the community living movement, these groups worked for the closure of institutions for people labelled as developmentally disabled. At the same time, governments concerned with fiscal restraint undertook vigorous downsizing exercises which led to the depopulation and, ultimately, closure of many large institutional facilities.

In the 1970s and 1980s, many people who might once have been placed in institutions started to live in the community. Here, the range of services that had previously been provided by a single institution was more dispersed. The potential existed for individuals and families to have more control over their services and to become actively involved in community life. However, when institutions started to close, relatively little was known about how to structure a decentralized system of community-based services in order to realize this vision. During the following thirty-year period of institutional closure and movement of people to the community, a variety of agency structures and service approaches evolved, in a rapid and often rather haphazard way. As a result, many services learned as they went along. Planning of services for community living often took place without input from the people who were directly affected—the individuals in the institutions themselves and their families. Community members were rarely part of the social support network that surrounded people who came out of institutions, especially during the early days of deinstitutionalization.

In many instances, services in the community functioned more as mini-institutions. The principles of practice that had shaped care in institutions were often carried over into community, with the result that residences in community were sometimes described as "institutions without walls." Adults with developmental disabilities continued to live in congregate settings, some relatively small with four to six residents in a group home, and others quite large, with up to 25 or 30 people in a residential setting. The majority of people's everyday needs for food, shelter, personal care, leisure and recreation, and vocational activity, were dealt with by one service provider or agency, still mostly under one roof. Government funding was given to transfer agencies, for the care of their "consumers" or "clients." Accordingly, funds these agencies received were channelled into programs that could serve people's collective needs.

As the system has evolved, the principles that guide it have become more explicit and, in some cases, entrenched. In an effort to chart the evolution of thinking on services and supports for people labelled as disabled, we focus on four philosophies and principles of service which are generally well known within the developmental disabilities service field and which we feel confident in suggesting are the dominant philosophies of practice in North America today. These are (a) "quality" service, (b) advocacy, (c) normalization/social role valorization, and (d) capacity building.

"Quality" service. One principle that guided the design of developmental services in the early years of deinstitutionalization was, not surprisingly, a transplanted version of an idea that had worked well for service providers in institutional settings. This philosophy of practice, the notion of quality service drawn primarily from the principles of organizational management, has continued to influence the design and delivery of community-based services to the present day. The sheer numbers of people needing community-based services during the first major wave of deinstitutionalization meant a rapid expansion of the service system. Many agencies thought they had to focus their attention on the managerial and administrative skills needed to run these complex service delivery organizations in ways that ensured "quality" care. Safety and the efficient delivery of quality services to people who had previously been virtually invisible in community settings became priorities for service providers. Service quality was seen to exist when agencies worked effectively within their budgets, to deliver services to people that ensured client safety and comfort. Accountability ultimately meant being able to ensure funders that their dollars were being managed effectively and dispersed in an efficient manner into programs which could serve the greatest number of people. It was these criteria, then, that were encapsulated in the notion of quality service. As a result, meeting individual needs and preferences was not identified as a central feature of quality service.

Services became more bureaucratized and in many instances distanced from the people they supported. McKnight (1987) described the resultant pattern as a hierarchy of managed service systems, in which individuals became consumers of the commodities produced by the human service systems, including needs assessments, service plans, protocols, and procedures. Services and budgets grew, and service providers responded to the pressures to demonstrate accountability by moving toward professionalization of services and support personnel, further distancing themselves from the individuals they were supporting. This gradually increasing emphasis on service management and efficiency has in many respects impeded the potential impact of the more value-oriented philosophies of normalization, social role valorization, and, more recently, capacity building.

Advocacy. We mentioned that agitation by parent groups was one of the factors that precipitated the deinstitutionalization movement of the 1950s and 1960s. Over time, these parent groups organized into groups like Associations for Community Living. Associations for Community Living have now become major service providers themselves in many Canadian communities, but they continue to define their role—to articulate their philosophy of service—in a way that includes advocacy (Dybwad, 1990). Parent-directed groups have continued to lobby for improvement in the service system. They have focussed on creating smaller and more personalized living arrangements and promoting community inclusion in the areas of leisure, school, and employment.

Advocacy has continued to be viewed as a critical aspect of human services and support to persons with disabilities, although there is considerable debate about the effectiveness of advocacy in promoting real change when it is often carried out by the more powerful on behalf of the less powerful. The case against advocacy suggests that it tends not to create change and in fact may exacerbate dependency. Nevertheless, the reality is that persons with disabilities have not been well served in terms of assurance of social justice and the privileges enjoyed by other members of society. Advocacy has been utilized in an attempt to ensure that people with disabilities are able to receive the sort of supports and services that will enable them to live decent lives alongside other people in the community. Over time, the emergence of self-advocates within the disability movement has played an important role in promoting the rights of people with disabilities and giving more prominence to the issues in terms of the public agenda (Shapiro, 1993). And in many instances, self-advocates have been able to work with other advocates to try to reduce the uncertainty that characterizes social support networks. Their persistent and determined efforts, first in terms of gaining access to support, and second, of ensuring continuity of support, are particularly important during a period when governments are seeking ways to reduce their budgets—which can be especially threatening for vulnerable people who depend on public funding to satisfy their most basic needs.

Normalization and social role valorization. Although institutional mindsets persisted in many community-based services, advocacy groups and families continued to lobby for approaches that would allow the system to realize its potential as a force for empowerment and full community integration. Partly because of their continued efforts, the normalization principle began to take hold as a philosophy of practice among service providers in the 1970s (Pedlar, 1990). Nirje conceived of normalization in terms of the "normal modes and rhythms of life and patterns of culture in any given environment" (1980, p.47). Integration into one's environment is essential to being part of the community and being able to participate in the normal rhythms and patterns of everyday life. Social role valorization (Wolfensberger, 1983; 1997), which emerged in the 1980s, elaborated and extended this theme. It provided a guiding framework for supporting people to develop valued social roles in community settings. It also sensitized advocates and service providers to the need to ensure that labelled people are afforded the full rights of citizenship.

The values embedded in these practice principles became very influential in the early 1980s, and contributed to a refocussing of developmental services. Some agencies began to look beyond the need to keep people safe, and asked how services could best incorporate training and development of people. This focus brought goals like individual growth and advancement to the fore. Normalization and social role valorization, then, provided much of the impetus for persons with disabilities to be more fully integrated as active, participating members of their communities. However, for a variety of reasons, normalization and social role valorization, in and of themselves, have not been able to ensure that service systems function in ways that ensure self-determination.

Capacity building. By the early 1980s, the valued roles that people with disabilities could play and the contribution they could make to society started to gain wider public attention. This new focus on broader quality of life indicators was more oriented toward individuals and their personal needs and interests (Hughes & Hwang, 1996; Schalock, 1997). The "capacity building" framework or philosophy of practice was based on the assumption that individual growth had more to do with building on the strengths and abilities that individuals had, and less to do with trying to "fix" their problems or minimize their limitations (Kretzman & McKnight, 1993; Mount, 1995). It challenged service providers to refocus their thinking on recognizing and building upon people's strengths—the "pluses" that already existed in an individual's life.

Not surprisingly, people with disabilities responded positively to the opportunity to develop and apply their skills and abilities. As a result, through the last decade, capacity building has been increasingly recognized as potentially progressive and helpful in promoting self-determination and enabling the individual to grow and enjoy the rewards of participation in community life (Bradley, 1994; Hutchison & McGill, 1998; Meyer, Peck, & Brown, 1991; Racino, 1992).

Philosophies of Practice That Drive Today's Services

The results of our quantitative survey provided extensive information concerning the kinds of agencies offering services to adults with developmental disabilities. Of the 801 agencies that responded to the survey, 688 (85.8%)

were from the non-profit sector; of these 186 (23.2%) indicated that they were part of the Association for Community Living; that is, the association which emerged from the parents' movement we talked about earlier in this chapter. The remaining 112 respondents, or 14.0%, represented private, for-profit agencies. Until quite recently one would not have expected to find anything but non-profit organizations involved in the provision of support services to persons with disabilities, so this 14% reflects a notable shift in human services in Canada. A defining characteristic of private, for-profit agencies is that they are not required to operate with a volunteer board of directors. Some do, but this is not required by law, as is the case with non-profit agencies which receive public funding.

The historical development of support services to adults with developmental disabilities has been influenced by a number of factors which reflect changing and emerging ideologies. However, the philosophies of practice we have reviewed here—quality service, advocacy, normalization or social role valorization, and capacity building—have played dominant roles in shaping the human services landscape. The data gathered in this study suggest that all four of these philosophies are still evident in the thinking behind services today.

Mandates or mission statements were provided by 737 of the 801 agencies that responded to the survey. These statements were analysed for content based on the four key philosophies, using a latent coding approach. This allowed us to identify and count key words and phrases (set out in chart 2, appendix I), which captured meanings embedded in the mission statement texts. Some mission statements contained reference to more than one of the four key philosophies. In these instances, the first-mentioned philosophy was taken as the dominant perspective, most likely to shape the structure and content of the service delivery. Service philosophies reflecting capacity building were contained in 28% of the mandate statements, normalization/social role valorization in 11%, and advocacy in 6%. But "quality" service, which was mentioned in 55% of the mandate statements, still seemed to dominate the support landscape. The pattern of distribution of philosophies of service was generally consistent across agency types, with the exception that advocacy was not cited by agencies that operate in the for-profit sector.

Approaches to Funding Services

A key factor in enhancing individual control and autonomy is the resources that are available to direct one's own care and support on an individualized basis. As social role valorization and capacity building philosophies began to take hold in the late 1980s, the idea of funding people, in contrast to funding programs, started to emerge as an important alternative approach to support.

Many service providers, families, self-advocates, and advocates sought ways of developing more person-centred approaches to social support. However, despite widespread enthusiasm for the idea of individualized planning and funding, concrete changes in approaches to services, most especially related to efforts to develop more person-centred support, lagged behind.

We asked agencies to indicate how their activities were funded. We identified four primary approaches to funding. First, there is the traditional approach through program funding used by transfer agencies, where funds are transferred to the agencies for specific programs, such as vocational, residential, recreational, and so on, with no dollar amounts being specifically allocated to individuals. Second, some funding occurs through global funding, where the agency may allocate funds from the program funding "pot," so to speak, to support individuals according to specific needs. A third, relatively innovative type of funding, is known as indirect individual funding, where the agency receives funds on behalf of an individual for his or her particular supports. The agency can then purchase services from a number of sources to meet what it perceives to be the individual's needs. Finally, the most recent effort to individualize support comes through direct individual funding, with funds being transferred directly to the control of the individual and/or his or her family, so that they may purchase services directly from service providers, as they so choose.

All four of these approaches to funding are practised in Canada. Since many agencies reported that they have adopted more than one funding approach, the number of funding approaches reported by the agencies (1,111) exceeds the number of reporting agencies (801). Program funding dominates. Five hundred and thirty-six (48.2%) of the funding approaches reported were instances of program funding; 253 (22.8%) were instances of indirect individualized funding; 167 (15.0%) were instances of global funding; 155 (14.0%) were instances of direct individualized funding. The distribution of these funding approaches across the country is indicated in appendix I, as are the operational definitions of the funding types used in the survey.

At the time our data were collected, the majority of the *direct* individualized funding for individuals with developmental disabilities was taking place in the western provinces of the country, particularly British Columbia and Alberta. Alberta has most clearly pursued policies geared to individualized funding; survey respondents from that province reported that 66% of their operations were conducted with direct individualized funding. A fair percentage of agencies too were engaged in *indirect* individualized funding, especially in Manitoba and Nova Scotia. Comments received from many agencies across the country indicated a definite interest in being able to operate with a more individualized approach to services, which individualized funding would facilitate. Important though is the realization that individualized funding does not negate the very real possibility that people will continue to be grouped according to their disability. This certainly became evident in the second phase of our work, when we visited individuals supported by these different approaches to funding. We will return to this consideration later.

Marching on the Spot or Moving Forward?

The changes in approaches to services, including efforts to develop more person-centred support, appear to have been relatively slow to emerge. This is likely explained at least in part by the fact that service providers simply have not known any way of providing support other than by grouping people together according to their disability. Service providers have a fairly solid record of establishing programs which, for all intents and purposes, have responded pretty well to people's needs for food and shelter and have given people something to occupy their working days and free time. It might be argued that people have not suffered living under these sorts of service arrangements. Services are, after all, community-based and have enabled people to be supported in the community rather than in institutions. But whether people have actually had an opportunity to reach their potential, whether their capacity for development has been enhanced, and whether they have flourished in these situations—these questions have not really been answered or even raised by researchers. Perhaps the reason they have not been raised is that the improvement in life quality for people in the community, after the stultifying conditions of many institutions, is undeniable. In recent years, though, self-advocates and others have begun suggesting that people are not doing as well as they might under existing community arrangements, and are looking for better ways to support people with developmental disabilities.

We know there were a number of developments from the 1960s to the 1990s when attempts were made to find alternative approaches to care. As we have already pointed out, one of these approaches, normalization, has a long and significant history in driving community living for persons with developmental disabilities. But in order to fully implement the normalization concept, sufficient funding must be allocated to permit development of adequate community-based services. Governments' preoccupation with deficit reduction and the concomitant privatization of human services over the past decade have resulted in a general downgrading of social concerns and a transfer of responsibility for the care of disadvantaged persons from the broader societal level to the family and local community. Serious attempts to implement the normalization principle have been hampered by fiscal restraints (Canadian Association for Community Living, 1998). Weaknesses appear in the system when individuals have only minimal income and no familial or other social supports at the community level (Lightman, 1986).

The privatization of care within the service-for-profit sector raises critical questions related to access to resources (Ashbaugh & Smith, 1996) and in fact, more than a decade ago, prompted Bercovici (1983) to ask whether it is "possible to carry out normalization policies with entrepreneurial caregivers" (p. 204). Similarly, the contradictions inherent within program-centred support services further limit the ability of the normalization and social role valorization frameworks to deliver on their promise of normalizing the environment of people with developmental disabilities, and ensuring that they come to occupy valued social roles. As Bradley (1994) commented, "the overriding values associated with normalization are still at war with the way in which service systems are organized, staffed, designed and funded" (p. 27).

The idea of funding people rather than programs started to catch people's attention in the late 1980s as more energy was focussed on individualized rather than collective support programs. Among the first approaches to individualized support was service brokerage (Salisbury, Dickey, & Crawford, 1987), where people who acted as service brokers sought out support services to accommodate a person's needs and strengths. This meant service brokers would purchase services from different providers who would then be involved in attempting to meet the person's various needs, rather than having all of the person's needs looked after by just one agency.

Other more individualized models of social support that have started to influence the human services landscape include innovations such as circles of support (Forsey, 1993; Wertheimer, 1995), support clusters (Ochocka, Roth, Lord, & Macnaughton, 1993), wraparound, and microboards (VanDenberg & Grealish, 1996; Women's Research Centre, 1994). "Microboard" is a term that appears often in this book as it was one of the approaches to support that we examined in some depth. When we talk about microboards though, we are more concerned with the ideas behind microboards than with microboards per se. The ideas behind microboards really tell us more about a way of providing social support to society's more vulnerable members, as will become apparent later. Briefly, a microboard consists of a small number of people, usually four to six, who collectively provide support to a person with a disability. These people may be family members, friends, advocates, and professionals, who have a strong understanding and knowledge of the person. What distinguishes the microboard from some of the other innovative ways of supporting people, like circles of support, is that the funding goes to the individual and the microboard; so while the microboard members offer informal support to the person, they also have the fiscal resources to obtain the more formal supports and services a person may need. Microboard members, in turn, are accountable to the individual, working with him or her in developing a life planning process, and determining the supports that will allow the person access to community life. Provincial funding goes, then, on an individualized basis directly to the individual and the management of these funds rests with the individual and his or her microboard. Microboards and the other innovations we have mentioned, share a commitment to cooperation and partnership among the individual with a disability, people who are paid to provide support, and people who are not paid and simply provide support to the individual as a friend or loved one. Many of these more individualized models emerged concurrently, suggesting that people have been keen to find more responsive approaches to social support, especially as the inadequacies of the more traditional approaches to serving people in congregate situations in the community have become more of an issue. Other work detailing the struggles service providers and individuals face in traditional services include Bogdan and Taylor (1994); Dowson (1991); Lord and Pedlar (1991); Singer and Powers (1993); Singer (1993); Taylor, Bogdan, and Lutfiyya (1995).

What we have been able to ascertain from the agencies in Canada that participated in the survey is that new ideologies and values are beginning to emerge. People's capacities are being recognized, and while agencies continue to see administration of their services as a primary goal, this is not incompatible with the related objective of ensuring a good quality of life for the people they support. Meanwhile, traditional program funding continues to dominate the support services landscape. When we embarked on this exploration, however, we were far from clear just what the implications of funding approaches were for individuals' lives. Neither were we willing to conclude that agencies which provided support to individuals who were funded directly would inevitably be more forward thinking in their philosophy of service than the more traditional agencies with their program-funded operations. Furthermore, we questioned whether direct payment of funding to the individual, who would then seek support from "the marketplace," would in itself guarantee personal autonomy and a shift from the "image of dependence." A balance needs to be attained, with responsible person-centred care and the best possible options being made available to the individual.

Certainly, individualized support and direct payments of funding to individuals with disabilities continue to be linked to empowerment by a number of social policy analysts and consumer representatives (Centre for Research and Education in Human Services, 1988; 1993; Laing 1991; Marlett, 1988; Morris, 1997; Roeher Institute, 1991; 1993a). It was in large part to probe this hypothesized linkage in more depth that in the second year of this study we visited several regions of Canada where we met on an individual basis with adults with developmental disabilities, with their families, and with service providers. Some of these participants were receiving individualized funding. As we were to learn, the experience of these people, and of their families and other support persons, is that direct funding leads to greater control over the resources that they are able to access; but this control is somewhat precarious.

As for realizing the dreams many hold for ensuring that people with disabilities are able to fully participate in society as respected and equal members, the pace at which changes in thinking and supporting people have occurred is slow. But as we discovered from our conversations with people in the second phase of our work, some individuals and families are gradually beginning to experience the potential of more person-centred approaches to funding and to support. This is a matter that we'll be looking at through the course of this book, especially in chapters 3-5. First though, we need to discuss the agencies that helped us reach the individuals who participated in the qualitative phase of the study. The characteristics of these agencies or study sites, as outlined below, will provide some contextual background to the accounts people gave us of their lives.

The Study Sites

As is often the case with studies of community life for persons with developmental disabilities, in order to reach participants, we were dependent upon agencies that provide services to them to facilitate a connection. The very fact that agencies played the "gatekeeper" role in connecting us to individuals and their families says something about the world of many individuals with a developmental disability. Over the course of 101 interviews, we met with 141 people—52 adults with developmental disabilities, 26 family members, and 63 others in a variety of front-line support and managerial roles. The full list of study participants, identified by pseudonym, is included in appendix II.

We wanted to learn about people's experiences with all of the dominant approaches to support across Canada. Thus, we included people supported by non-profit agencies, public and private, as well as by agencies that represented the private, for-profit sector. Also important was the inclusion of representatives of the traditional parent association, now recognized as the Association for Community Living. In meeting study participants for the second phase of this work, then, we visited four microboards, one private non-profit agency, two private for-profit, and three public non-profit support agencies. These agencies were located in five different regions of Canada, from the east, central, and western provinces.

Microboards. Four microboards participated in the study. They were all structured in somewhat similar ways, but with differences that reflect the flexibility of this approach to delivering service. Each board served one individual and provided support to that person according to his or her needs, preferences, and capacities. The microboards also acted as the administrative and managerial body for services to the individual, who was funded directly from the provincial government; that is, funds for the person's care were channelled directly to the microboard, which was responsible for putting together a budget to cover administration, the securing of services, and the person's care. The members, along with the individual, were responsible for hiring staff. These arrangements reflect the fact that microboards carry out the functions generally handled by agency management. The intent is to have sufficient members to ensure balance and range of support from the membership. Microboards generally comprise four to six people, including the individual him or herself, along with family members, parents and siblings or other relatives, friends, and other people perhaps, who know the individual in some professional capacity, such as a health care provider or teacher.

Microboards first emerged in response to a desire to individualize support, especially in the case of people with more complex developmental disabilities, and those labelled medically fragile. The four adults who participated in the study had fairly complex disabilities. Their microboards had been in operation from one to three years. Three of the four individuals had or were soon to have their own home or apartment. One was living in the home of his parents at the time we met, but plans were underway to build a small home at the back of the parents' property, where the individual would then live. None of these people had been placed in an institution at any time. Two had had earlier short and not very successful stays in group homes. At the time of the study, all four microboards had close contact with a provincial government employee, called a facilitator, who provided a link between the individual and the funding ministry.

Private, for-profit agencies. One of the two private, for-profit agencies that participated in the study offered a range of services to people who were described as "falling through the cracks," in that there were no traditional services in place to support their specific needs. Some of these people had spent time in institutions. The owner/operator employed staff who were assigned to work with individuals in a range of capacities, generally to serve as a stepping stone for people who needed some interim support or training for three to six months. For instance, they assisted individuals in life skills development, in obtaining employment, in seeking out leisure time pursuits, in connecting with services and activities in their community, or in finding housing. The bulk of the agency's operations were funded by clients' indirect individual funding, with a smaller percentage coming from the province as global funding.

The second private, for-profit organization that we visited had an advisory board and in this respect functioned more typically along the lines of a traditional community-based human service agency. The agency supported individuals who received direct dollars from the province. While called direct individualized funding, this is perhaps a little misleading in that all recipients received the same fixed amount each month. Many of these people had once lived in institutions. In this region, persons labelled developmentally disabled are assigned a public trustee through whom decisions regarding their support, including funding and expenditures, are channelled. The agency subcontracted to private home providers, who acted as live-in companions and provided support.

Private, non-profit agencies. The private, non-profit agency that participated in this study was part of a much larger international organization which supported persons with disabilities across Canada and beyond. The relationship that the agency had with the people it supported was more family-like than one generally finds in traditional human service agencies. While support occurred essentially from within the confines of the agency, residences housing persons with disabilities, along with non-disabled peers and workers, were located throughout the community at large. Some individuals worked in the community while others were employed in sheltered employment which was operated by the agency. Funded primarily by program, a defining characteristic of the vision of this agency was its strong spiritual base.

Public, non-profit agencies. All three public, non-profit agencies were organized in ways that reflect the dominant service model to persons with developmental disabilities. They served some individuals who had lived in the community all their lives, and others who had spent varying amounts of time in institutions. These agencies were closely aligned with the local Associations for Community Living. The agencies' services were principally funded by program, with some global funding and indirect individualized funding arrangements in place. Two of the agencies provided residential, vocational, and leisure time services. The third provided only residential services. The day-to-day service practices varied between agencies, but it was most often the case that individuals had a key worker or primary support person who was closely associated with that person. These workers were more often appointed to a residence, though, not a person, so that a person who lived in a particular house would be supported by one of the workers employed in that house. As we shall see from the things people told us, while they might not have had any choice as to which staff supported them, many developed strong bonds with these workers.

A Note on the Qualitative Study and Emerging Theory

Theory derived from qualitative research aims to provide understanding. The second phase of our work allowed us to enter the lives of individuals, and to gain understanding from them of their life experiences. Of particular concern were the ways in which people experienced support in relation to a sense of empowerment. However, we approached this inductively, not deductively as one would with quantitatively derived theory. Although, as pointed out earlier, from the inception of this work we were obviously sensitized to various concepts that pertain to empowerment, we did not enter these individuals' lives with a theory of empowerment which we wanted to test. We wanted to learn from them what their experiences of support were and how that was understood. The word empowerment was not used in our interviews. Instead, people talked about their life experiences and analysis of their narratives led to an understanding of what empowerment meant in their lives.

In the process of analysis and interpretation of people's narratives, we came together as field researchers after field visits, collectively considered the narratives, and began the process of category identification through constant comparison between and across data (Glaser and Strauss, 1967). The four stages of the constant comparison method were applied to our data: (1) comparing incidents, (2) integrating categories, (3) delimiting the theory, and (4) writing the theory. The use of the term "categories" in data analysis is worth mentioning here. Categories in qualitative work do not parallel categories in quantitative work; in the former instance, categories allow the researcher to place data items together with other data items that "seem to help describe something" (Kirby & McKenna, 1989, p.130). Thus, qualitative work is able to tolerate ambiguity in a way that quantitative research cannot (Morse, 1997). Quantitative research requires that categories offer precise definitions of specified variables which are clearly identified from existing theory prior to starting out on a new research endeavour. Quantitative research offers description, explanation and prediction related to a perhaps very specific part of that existing theory. That is its purpose. In contrast, the purpose of qualitative research is to unearth meaning and offer a depth of understanding that is unrealistic to expect from quantifiable data. In fact, qualitative data resists quantification and its trustworthiness rests in large part on its ability to provide rich and detailed descriptions which help us make sense of the meaning of social phenomena.

The qualitative method allows that confirmation occurs in the process of theory development as the researcher "takes apart the story" within the data, continuing with constant comparison across categories essentially until saturation is reached; that is, until an incident adds nothing more to our understanding, or, if you like, to the emerging theory. We were able to experience this in our study inasmuch as when the theory "solidified," fewer and fewer modifications or additional or new properties were evident in the data, indicating theoretical saturation. Thus, as the constant comparison continued throughout the theory development process, we began to exercise parsimony of variables, as data were distilled and uniformities were identified across categories. This in turn allowed for concentration and reduction of the initial set of categories and the formulation of theory with a smaller set of higher level concepts. Hence, theory was delimited (Glaser & Strauss, pp.108-11). In our case, the higher level concepts of mutuality and texture were associated with a social ecology theory of empowerment, which is the subject of chapter 6.

Voices of the Study Participants

The data we gathered in this study are vast and rich and provided us with a level of understanding which is really only possible through the sorts of in-depth interviews we had with people. Thus, it was a deliberate decision on our part to use the voices of the individuals with a disability and those around them to illustrate the sorts of lives people have: where they live, how they spend their free time, and how they feel about their work and relationships with family, staff, and friends. Chapters 3, 4, and 5 specifically set out people's thoughts, reflections, and responses to their life experiences. Rather than paraphrase or recast what they told us, we wanted their stories to be told in their own words. In this way we hoped to provide a deeper understanding of the lived experiences of these men and women. We think this was a good decision—it is through the study participants' own words that we are best able to capture their perceptions and perspectives, and, in turn, illustrate which approaches to supporting people appear most promising for enhancing the richness and texture of daily life. We hope you will see this for yourselves as you read on.

Chapter 3

FAMILY AND HOME LIFE

Our efforts to understand texture in the lives of people with developmental disabilities begin with an exploration of aspects of everyday life that most profoundly affect our general well-being—our home and family life. In recent years, researchers have begun to understand the dynamics within families that include a member with a disability, and to understand the family as an interconnected system. Families with children who have disabilities have faced extraordinary challenges in the past concerning the institutionalization imperative that characterized much of the support services up to the latter part of this century. With the more recent deinstitutionalization movement, some of these parents have been reunited with their adult children. Families who kept their children at home faced another set of challenges as they sought out alternative living situations in the community for their adult sons and daughters. Family was significant to most people with whom we met, even when there had been little or no contact for many years. Where family involvement existed, it was generally frequent and intense. Where it was absent, staff often expressed concern and disappointment on behalf of the individual. Some acted as surrogate families, and attempted to include the individual in their own family ventures. It is also the case that the families of many of our study participants were no longer intact and so people saw their parents in different settings and at different times.

People's families and people's homes figured prominently in the stories they told us about their lives. For those who did not live with their families, and that was the majority in the case of the people with whom we met, the group home continued to be the dominant form of housing for people with developmental disabilities. However, as we and other researchers have noted, attempts are being made across the service system to find alternative models of residences for individuals. Many of these models provide people with homes that more closely resemble those of people who do not have disabilities. Smaller numbers of adults live together in apartments or houses, for example, as members of an unrelated family where support is provided. However, these structurally more normative housing situations do not necessarily lead to lifestyles that include more control, more integration, or more texture. As was evident from what we learned, finding a satisfactory home is difficult for people with disabilities and their family members, for a variety of reasons, many of which will be evident in the following excerpts from conversations with people in this study. First, though, we consider something of the relationships between the family and the individual.

Families

Valuing and Caring for Family Members Who Have Disabilities

There were different ways in which families demonstrated care and valuing of the individuals who were part of this study. Not infrequently, parents or other family members committed much time and energy to trying to ensure that their relative was well cared for, was receiving appropriate support, and continued to live as a valued member of the family.

Janet, Sarah's mother
We've been married for thirty years and Sarah is our youngest child. She was twenty-three in March and she has been an individual that we have cherished greatly but we made a commitment to her life a long time ago which really altered our life. And it was, I think when she was younger because of her many facets of her disability, there were so many things that she couldn't do. We tried to include her in everything in our lives. But because of her problems with her physical disabilities that sort of go along with all the other stuff, she couldn't do a lot of things, like her instability, her problem with her apraxia and her lack of balance. We stopped camping and stopped canoeing and all those kinds of things because it was a real problem for Sarah and she was not able to walk very far, whatever. So what happened was my son and my husband pursued you know sort of all those kinds of things. And although I like those things I felt no resentment to sort of stay home, as long as they were doing it. And read and did a lot of those things. But you know it really changed. We found that we were kind of happy prisoners in our own home.
(Public, non-profit agency)

A major concern for many families was ensuring that their son or daughter would have care once they were no longer able to support him or her.

Sadie, Chad's mother
I want to see Chad happy. That's the main thing for me. Sure I would like to see, his goal is that he can get a job. And support himself. I would like to see that he did get better and better and better and he can support himself. Half

*way, you know. And that he's happy where he's living and what he's doing.
And when I am gone that somebody will be there.*
(Private, for-profit agency)

Occasionally, older parents refused to secure additional support for their
son or daughter outside the family. In speaking of her three sisters who were
developmentally disabled, one woman explained why it was difficult for her
family to go outside the family for help, both in terms of the disability pension
to which her sisters were entitled, and in terms of seeking residential support
beyond the family:

Jen, Geraldine's sister
*When they were younger my brother said that they should be getting a pension
for disability. They never got that pension until 10 years before my dad died.
I said what happens when you aren't here. He said they're my children and
I'm going to look after them. But he eventually did allow them to have it and
they should have it, they're entitled to it. Once they got their pensions they
were able to have a lot more, it increased their quality of life. If we were
millionaires then it would be different, but with the family we had . . . we had
a nice house and food and stuff. But you know that there are a lot of people of
my dad's generation that are the same. . . . I think that it's hard on older
people. My father would have never done this. He was worried what was
going to happen when he was gone. He wanted me to sign papers saying I
would never ever put them anywhere. I said I couldn't do it because I didn't
know what the future held. I said to him what is going to happen to them, no
one else in the family thinks they can do it. But I know that if he could see the
program now he would be happy. What this program does is gives us the
closeness to them without them being with us.*
(Public, non-profit agency)

Intense Involvement. Parents differed in their involvement in the day-to-day
life of their adult son or daughter once they had obtained caregiving
arrangements outside the family. For many whose children had more complex
disabilities, they felt it imperative that they maintain very close control and
monitored every aspect of care:

Bev, with her mother, Jill, and live-in caregiver, Judy
*Q: Bev, did you want to live with Judy?
Jill: It was better than [the institution], right? Yes. [responds for Bev].
Judy: It wasn't her choice, it was mom's [Jill's] choice. Bev was living in [the
institution] and mom wanted her closer to home. And I met her through a
broker and we just took steps from there. And then she came for visits for a
month, weekend visits. And then she moved in with me after a month of
weekend visits full-time.*

Q: Jill, when you were looking for a change from her previous arrangement, did you try, did you show her different places, or did you look at different places?
Jill: I looked at them, because I raised her and I knew what she was capable of and what she needed.
(Private, for-profit agency)

Many parents ensured that even when their adult children had left home, they were involved in essentially every aspect of their day-to-day lives and, in fact, some families took on a particularly protective role:

Ann, with her mother, Cynthia
Q: Who helped you make up your schedule?
Ann: Mom did . . . with the groceries.
Cynthia: We help her get the groceries. I take her every month to get groceries. She eats and buys what she wants.
Q: What about on the weekends? What do you do?
Cynthia: Who do you go to visit?
Ann: Grandmother.
Cynthia: Who else?
Ann: Mom and Dad.
Cynthia: That's about it, she's not one to have lots of friends. She doesn't really like to have friends, and I like it that way. She's just learned to be happy with herself. So she's content to be at home with herself.
(Public, non-profit agency)

Less Involvement. For people like Ann, the family was not simply the focal point of the individual's world, but rather it *was* their world. In other instances, however, when the adult son or daughter left home and became part of a formal residential service, families stepped out of their lives. The number of disrupted families indicated to us something of the stresses and strains that families faced. This conversation suggests family is important to many people, even though the amount of contact may be minimal:

Keith
Q: Do you get together with your dad?
Yeah, two years ago I did.
Q: And you have one sister in Australia, do you have any other brothers and sisters?
I have only one sister and five brothers. My mom lives in [adjacent county], and my brother . . . he spent some time last year, he took me to visit my mom in my mom's house.
(Public, non-profit agency)

When marriages end, or parents remarry, new stressors emerge:

Sandy, support worker to Keith
Sandy: He has four brothers, one sister and mom and dad. His dad used to be involved a lot, but his dad just met a new lady, so his time is cut down. This is frustrating to him. Mom sees Keith occasionally, two times a year, but they do a lot of phone contact between mom and dad and [his sister]. He doesn't see his other brothers a lot because they live close to his mom's.
Q: Does he initiate contact?
Sandy: Keith will say I like to call my mom, or my dad. Or he will say, "Mother's Day is coming up and I would like to buy a card," and then I will assist him with braille for the card.
(Public, non-profit agency)

Holiday times signalled particular tensions around family contact. Staff became sensitive to the involvement of family members on those occasions traditionally considered "family time." There was often ambiguity around whether or not the family would involve the individual in traditional celebrations. For example, in Steve's case, his worker noted that while his family may have made contact around these special occasions, they seemed to feel their responsibility essentially ended there, that is, in ascertaining that he had some place to go for the holidays. It was unclear whether they would actually include him in their family gathering if he did not have a place to go and if he were to be alone:

Karen, support worker to Steve
Q: So they may or may not initiate contact?
Karen: Yes, they are the ones that do initiate contact. Steve doesn't call anybody. But when there is a special occasion like Father's Day or Christmas they will call to make sure that he has a place to go. Because I find that they feel that's their responsibility. If he had a place to go then they'd say fine but they wouldn't invite him to the family thing.
(Public, non-profit agency)

Perhaps, not surprisingly, the role staff played varied in such situations. Some saw themselves as having a role in rebuilding or developing that link back to the family, while others took a more passive stance, but at the same time provided moral support to the person whose contact with family appeared to have disintegrated:

Donna, support worker to Judy
Q: Is there contact with family?
Donna: I really don't have a great handle on it myself. I ask Judy because periodically she will talk to her dad but I don't think it's great contact that she

*has with him. I know different times he says that he would come down but he
never does.*
(Public, non-profit agency)

An uncertain future. The uncertainty that faced families regarding the future
security of their son or daughter, especially as the parents aged, cut across the
entire service system. One older mother explained her fears:

Adie, Harry's mother
Q: So, you're pretty happy with his living situation?
*Adie: I think about all the cutbacks, and I don't know what to do. If he
couldn't be there I would have to bring him home, I couldn't let him go into an
institution. It's the only worry I have. That's all I think about is Harry. He
needs someone. From what I understand, if they don't have someone to keep
an eye out for them, it's not the same for someone if they don't have parents or
someone to bring them home once in a while.*
(Private, for-profit agency)

When families had managed to put in place a system of care beyond the
traditional service system, such as was the case with people supported by
microboards, the most individualized and autonomous of the systems we saw,
the question of stability and continuity of support as the parents aged continued
to be an issue:

Colin and his microboard
*Q: I guess another thing [is] that parents and families age, and as they become
older themselves, and think of the future, what kind of difference would this
have made for you?*
Cory: Well, it's been a real concern of ours.
*Henry: Yeah, this is our next step. To figure out how we can carry on, if
anything happens to us or when it does. There is an organization . . . and they
try and set up the things, formalized, you pay for it, and they do actually what's
been happening to us, and help a parent organize, assist the parent through the
planning, all the way, if they need people around, to carry on after, then a
facilitator will help them and encourage them to get that, to get the friends, if
you don't have family around, or get an organization behind you, prepared to
take over.*
*Q: So the microboard principle would still exist then, if family members
themselves became unwell or unable to participate down the road?*
Henry: Yes.
*Cory: Ideally, yes. Our microboard, well, it's our fault. We haven't been very
diligent in getting together as a whole board.*
*Henry: And getting more members on it, maybe it's because our family, or our
personal friendships haven't been that wide, and with handicapped people you
might find that in a lot of families, that they've just had to reduce the number*

*of their personal friends due to the commitments at home. But we're hoping
to get a facilitator in the area. There's a pilot project going on in [town], so
we may try to take advantage of that and see how it goes. But that's a paid
service, you pay for it. We've actually been through part of the procedure with
our ministry worker and so we know what can happen.*
(Microboard)

Concerns about the future were certainly exacerbated by the guilt experienced
by many parents who felt they had given up a significant portion of the
parenting role. Dilon's mother talked about how she tried to deal with feelings
of guilt stemming from the fact that her son was now receiving care from a
public agency where staff shared in the parenting role for her son:

Ellen, Dilon's mother
*They [staff] are filling the space that I filled for 15 years. We're all sharing
a parenting role. I think you need to work things out so that you can work with
them. I think that if you think of it as their doing it because I can't, that gives
a whole lot of negative feelings. But I don't. I think of it as a parenting role
shared. I try not to let "the big G" get in the way, guilt.*
(Public, non-profit agency)

Clearly, long after adult children had left home, parental involvement was
important. Those who were able to advocate did so and invariably this was
significant in terms of people's support. Not all parents were so thoroughly
connected to the adult children, however, and not all connected families were
able to be active advocates. It was more difficult for parents whose children
had been institutionalized to take up the role of active advocate once the family
member returned to the community as an adult. Advocacy that had been so
central to the parent movement required energy and collective commitment.
Regardless of the support structure people were served by, the issue of aging
was relevant to the ability of family members to continue that advocacy.
Again, Colin's father, Henry, talked about the planning he was involved in in
relation to ongoing support for his son.

Henry, Colin's father
*I'm involved with the group in [town] that's trying it, because I've seen what's
happening with families in the association here, we all get old. What I could
see is exchanging, sitting on another microboard, and exchanging seats, sort
of sharing with another family, as long as it didn't take too much time, but then
it's trying to get younger families in, because we'll all grow old together.*
(Microboard)

Betsy's story provides another example of the significant role parents often find themselves playing on an ongoing basis. Her parents located a residential arrangement that they felt would offer her a place to call home after they were no longer able to care for her. They found a supported apartment arrangement where she ultimately lived alone, with occasional paid support from agency staff, along with more regular support from her mother. While the family felt Betsy needed more support, the move to an apartment marked the transition towards greater independence for her and gave some reassurance to the parents about a future in which she would ultimately be able to manage without them:

> Susan, Betsy's mother
> *Q: How was it decided that she move out?*
> *It was our idea. I knew when we were no longer here she would have to find somewhere to live, and a group home is not the place for her, so we put her in the apartment program. She's been alone since the last of April because her live-in left.*
> *Q: She's there all by herself? How's it working out?*
> *She's not very good with money. When she lived at home she always had enough money, but when she went to the apartment she didn't have nearly as much. She can't handle money, the live-in usually handles all of that.*
> *Q: So the live-in is needed for that then?*
> *Yes, and she needs company, to go grocery shopping with, to go to the mall with, or for walks or whatever.*
> *Q: How do you feel about her living situation? Do you feel happy?*
> *Oh yes. We're not gonna live forever. The doctor years ago said, "Don't keep her at home until something happens to you." We took his advice. She agreed to have her own apartment. So one Friday we said we would pick her up from work and take her [to the country] where we have a cottage, and she said, "No, I'm going to my own apartment." This isn't her home anymore.*
> (Public, non-profit agency)

The history of the parent movement demonstrates how extraordinarily hard families have had to work to gain recognition of the rights and entitlements of their sons and daughters, and brothers and sisters. What people said to us shows persuasively how important family involvement continues to be in relation to these rights and a secure future. Bit by bit, Betsy and her family and Colin and his family had gained some sense of what the future might look like. Others, too, felt they at least had an understanding of what needed to be done to secure "a place" in the community. What we learned from our conversations with individuals, family members, and staff was that family involvement for many is rich and rewarding in itself, but it can also be a necessary precursor to achieving goals in other spheres of people's lives. It was clear that family involvement could enhance texture in one's life. But it is paradoxical that in some instances, the concerns family had for their adult sons and daughters, most especially when they faced a particularly uncertain future, could also serve to diminish people's sense of competence and control. This paradox becomes more explicit later when we talk with people about their working day and the relationships they had with the individuals they cared for and the people who cared for them.

Group Homes

A Place Called Home

As a result of the apparent fragility of the service system, including the availability of a secure home for their family member, it seemed that abandonment by service providers and others was an enduring fear for many families. As Henry's comment about planning for the future suggests, no guarantees of a secure future seemed to exist for families. Meanwhile, many parents worked hard to see that their family member had a place to live, beyond the parental home.

Once the decision had been made to seek a home within the traditional service system, the path to community living typically led families and individuals to the group home. Earlier we provided a sketch of the ways in which group homes evolved during the initial years of the deinstitutionalization movement. Understanding this evolution and the philosophy that drove it remains important to the present day. Group homes are still the most common form of housing services for adults with developmental disabilities. Colin's parents provide some insight into how families end up at the door of a group home when seeking a place for their family member to live.

Colin and his microboard
Cory: It was the only route here really. I know group homes aren't for everybody but it seemed to be something Colin would like, he's very sociable, he likes lots of people around him. There were difficulties came up, one being that everyone that was working in the workshop and being looked after as such came under Ministry of Social Services at that time and Colin alone came under the umbrella of Ministry of Health and it was a bit like oil and water to try and mix the two. There were lots of difficulties with that situation. However, it seemed like it was going to work out. First of all he went to respite care for three or four days a week for a few months within the group home that he was going to move into. Meanwhile we went through the process of the paperwork and all to get him from our home to there permanently and during that time the whole administration of the Association for Community Living just fell apart for a lot of reasons—financial, management, labour—for a

whole lot of reasons, and it really collapsed three days before Colin was
supposed to move into the group home.
(Microboard)

Criticism of group homes is not new. Some have been described as
miniature institutions, as places where traditional philosophies like quality
service have been sustained. While our findings certainly showed that these
criticisms are often warranted, they also highlighted some of the complexities
that help to explain the perseverance of this model. We will look at some of
the issues that lead us to suggest that group home living can be a significant
barrier to the development of more textured lives for people with disabilities.

Disability Determines Grouping in Group Homes

The complexity of people's disability often acted as a determinant of where
and with whom people lived. As is well known in the service delivery field,
the tendency is to group people who have a similar disability. For instance,
people who are non-verbal or who use wheelchairs will find themselves in
residences along with others in similar situations. However, individuals and
staff are often aware that this offers people a less than desirable home situation:

Eli, support worker to Jack
I think as Jack gets older he's going to have more health problems. I would
like to see Jack happily married to his fiancée. Not even married, even just
living together. I would be for that. I would definitely like to see him not
living where he is now. I think there is too many people there. That is not a
put down to the staff, there's only one staff there for six people, all in
wheelchairs. I'd like to see him in a smaller place.
(Public, non-profit agency)

While staff and family members may recognize that there were potential
problems with grouping this way, the priority remained functional and
administrative. As well, from a staffing viewpoint and the availability of
supports, it was often economic considerations which drove the decision-
making process. Houses and staffing arrangements were essentially organized
as "programs." Indeed, that was how funding of services to traditional support
agencies was structured. Policies established way beyond the offices of the
agency determined how things played out in delivering services. One senior
manager explained the process to us:

Marlene, agency management
An individual is referred to us and we do an initial assessment, a functional assessment. We meet with the family members and the client to get an overview of the needs. We will then attempt to plan a service around that individual in conjunction with the consideration of others, because no service stands alone. Generally there are three people that live together except the group homes, but we haven't opened them since '85. So we look for people that may have needs met in a similar way and then establish a home, even down to the furniture, based on those people.
(Public, non-profit agency)

Roger, who is non-verbal and non-ambulatory, lived in such a home. His support worker, Pauline, talked with us on his behalf.

Pauline, support worker to Roger
Roger lives in a group home. He has four other housemates besides himself, so that is five individuals within our home. He is the only male in the house, the only male individual, the other four are ladies. I'm not really sure if it would be his choice to be there, his being the only male, it seems to be the other individuals in that home are also in wheelchairs and aren't verbal and so, I'm not sure if it's easier. It's hard to say because that is the only home that they don't come to the workshop during the day. Because it is a more high care group home than the other group homes. The individuals seem to be more independent in the other homes, so I'm not sure if that would be his choice but that is where he is because of the situations that arise. That is what my understanding is or what my feelings are.
(Public, non-profit agency)

Just a Place to Live, Not a Home

While everyone with whom we met lived in quite comfortable neighbour-hoods, in secure and decent housing, the people in group homes tended to talk about their residential situation as though it were simply a place to live, rather than their *home*. The group home as a residential option was not something people felt to be the optimal living arrangement. However, people confronted very real problems if they expressed a desire to move from the group home. They faced barriers in trying to relocate, partly as a result of the minimal options that were available, and partly as a result of funding arrangements which allocated money to residential programs rather than to individuals. At the same time, for many families and individuals who had experienced institutions, there was an enormous sense of gratitude simply being in a community setting, group home or not. One father talked about the years two of his sons, Roger and Lloyd, were in institutions:

Don, Roger's father
When we went to [the institution], I asked at the desk, "I am the father of Lloyd," and I had to wait a half hour, [for them] to make him presentable. I never seen his place. I'm glad that things have improved a lot [for Roger], his care. At that time he was on so many drugs, when he went to [another institution], all the medicines were dropped. His brother [Lloyd] joined him there. [The second place] was private. His brother [Lloyd] died there.
(Public, non-profit agency)

After years of struggle, the move to the community was very much welcomed by this family. Having been for years essentially on the "outside" of their children's lives, the idea of insisting on choosing where their one son was to live following deinstitutionalization was not something they were likely to pursue:

Don, Roger's father
Q: When Roger came from [the institution], did you have a choice of where he would live?
Don: The house was not there yet, it had to be built. But I didn't have any choice, but I felt it was a good place. . . . We feel that is privileged to go in there when there are so many others on the list.
(Public, non-profit agency)

For Roger the group home was indeed a place to live and for that his family was grateful. It was clearly better than the institution. Chris, in contrast, had lived all his life in the community, and his sister talked about her brother's life in a group home:

Rhonda, Chris's sister
Q: How long has he lived there?
I think he's been there four years, but he's been in a group home atmospheres since he was 18 years old, and he's 33, so 15 years.
Q: So you say he wanted to move?
It's because of problems in the home. It's in the relationship with the guys at the house right now. There used to be some women there, not quite so bad at that time, but now that there's just the guys and they have mostly lady counsellors and so I think there is a lot of competition. And also Steven who lives there requires a lot more attention and sometimes Bernie [another of the men] does things that upsets all the other guys. So that's when it all goes off and that's when we get the calls to say "I'm moving out."
Q: It's a tough one, when the relationships in the house get difficult. To find four compatible people ain't that easy?
No, I'm sure it isn't. They did have an okay situation before and when Bernie arrived, that's when everything erupted, and it's never been good since. And

we've expressed our opinions to [the manager] as well. We feel that this is his
home. It's supposed to be his home. In your home you're not unhappy.
(Public, non-profit agency)

Keith also found himself in a less than happy situation in his group home, but
he had come to accept this as his "lot," so to speak:

Keith
I live in a house at [street]. I've been living there almost for eight years.
Q: Is that a house with other people?
It's with gentlemen, and one of the staff is there too.
Q: Are these gentlemen your friends?
Well, Adi, sometimes when I go past him, he sometimes doesn't know what he
is doing to me and I can't see, so I feel him. I'm not too fussy about him.
Q: So do you tell him if you don't like something?
No, because I don't like when he punches me.
Q: So he's not your favourite person by the sounds of it?
No.
Q: So you have lived there for a number of years, and you live with these other
gentlemen. Would you say you like living there?
I am used to it, it's okay.
Q: Do you think there is somewhere else you'd rather live?
I don't know.
(Supported by public, non-profit agency)

Life in this group home was not unique in that it was fairly chaotic and
occasionally difficult for residents and staff. When people faced difficulties
with staff, they hesitated to take action for fear of reprisal, as suggested by
Jack's experience:

Jack
Q: How about your general situation, personally?
Some of my staff, I don't like at the house. When she's not on duty she'll go
into our rooms, lay down and go to sleep.
Q: Did you complain about that?
Yeah, then I got into shit 'cause I did.
Q: And they told her not to do that?
They come around and checked and see what she does.
Q: Is there any staff you can tell?
Yes, my friend [staff person].
Q: Is she good?
Yep, she writes everything down.
Q: So do you feel like you are the boss in that situation?
I think I am. Not when she comes in the house.
(Public, non-profit agency)

Other stories we heard indicated just how torn individuals and family members can be in terms of actually being able to act on the knowledge that something may be amiss. Families had so few options that they were very uncertain where their relative would go if attempts were made to change residences, with the result that most often they had to rationalize or ignore signs of discontent or unhappiness:

Adie, Harry's mother
Q: What about his current situation; is he happy there?
He is, but he always wants to come home. He really doesn't want go back [to the group home] . . . it's just him, he's comfortable at home. He's fairly happy, because when you go back with him he goes right into his room. This is what I can't understand, why he doesn't want to go back.
(Public, non-profit agency)

A disturbing implication of this lack of choice and need for as secure an arrangement as possible is that families may have considered it too great a risk to encourage their son or daughter to think about alternatives to the group home, or to become more involved in planning for their future. Consequently, staff or family members essentially controlled decisions around accommodation. It is important to recognize, nevertheless, that group homes have responded to the very real need for decent housing that existed and still exists in many of our communities. They allowed people who were formerly in institutions to come one step closer to living more normal lives in everyday residential settings. They enabled other people who had grown up with their families to take that first step toward adult life in a home with other adults. And for some families they offered a solution to extremely difficult circumstances. When all is said and done, though, a home ought to be more than a roof over people's heads. But typically this is all group homes have been; they have not been experienced as a *home*. There are, of course, group homes that truly function well, where people who like each other live and flourish. Sadly, these are relatively few in number.

In chapter 1 we introduced the idea of empowerment-in-community to suggest that it is especially by entering into affective and productive relations with others that a person becomes empowered. In part, this theme is intended to counteract the view that an empowered person is like a citadel that stands alone, dominating and self-sufficient. The group homes where Roger, Chris, Jack, and Harry lived succeeded to the extent that they put roofs over their heads. But, partly because residents were grouped on the basis of having similar disabilities, and had little or no say in determining who they would be living with, Roger, Chris, Jack, and Harry did not appear to experience much in the way of affective and productive relations with others in their group homes. And they did not flourish there. Their group homes failed to the extent that they did not form *homes*. This illustrates and somewhat confirms the theme of empowerment-in-community. The relative absence of affective and productive relations with others, of community, in many group homes helps explain why the residents do not find them empowering.

Alternatives to Group Homes

There are families across the country who have found ways to create more homelike living arrangements for their family member. Family Home and similar residential arrangements are an interesting alternative to the group home. Living independently, in one's own home or in an apartment, is a dream that has been realized by a few Canadians with developmental disabilities, but only when family support, funding structures, and service arrangements have been able to work together from a common, empowerment-driven paradigm. In our exploration of alternatives, we considered whether changes in the social and physical structure of the home appeared to lead to increased control for the individual.

Norma, who was engaged to Jack, lived alone in an apartment where she received support from a worker employed by a service agency's residential program. Norma and Jack hoped one day to be able to have their own place, but when we met her she was living in what is described as a supported independent living apartment program. We asked her how she found the apartment:

> Norma
> *Q:Was [the apartment] your choice?*
> Yes. [Staff] has an office and he looks at different apartments for certain people.
> *Q: And so with the things that you have in your apartment, were you able to choose how to furnish it?*
> Yeah, my dad helped me. We bought a sofa bed and it fits good, and we took the other one out.
> (Public, non-profit agency)

Later, we spoke with Stephanie, Norma's support worker, about the process of locating an apartment:

> Stephanie, support worker to Norma
> *Q: Do you know what the deciding factor was in terms of the place she is in now?*

*No, I have only taken over Norma's case for two years. Probably because it
was closer to the . . . workshop and the bus route.*
(Public, non-profit agency)

What appeared to be the driving force in the decision to move was the
convenience of the location. Although clearly location is an important
consideration, one might question whether Norma actually had much of an
opportunity to exercise choice in where she would live. With the change in
staff that went along with the move to the apartment, there was perhaps a lack
of continuity in terms of understanding the contextual background in Norma's
life. While she lived relatively independently, it was not evident that she was
living life quite as she would were she free to choose. The rationale the
support worker provided for the move suggested that a priority in the decision-
making process was to meet Norma's needs in a high quality, efficient way—a
perspective consistent with a quality service philosophy which, we suggest, is
fairly pervasive in the support services landscape.

Changing housing arrangements is not in and of itself enough to improve
quality of life. Barbara's story below demonstrated how more individualized
funding arrangements can open up opportunities for input into choice of living
situations. Barbara received indirect individualized funding through a for-
profit agency, but it still was not easy for her to either complain or move out
of an unsatisfactory residential setting. People without access to strong
advocacy services can rarely exert control over their residential situation.
Barbara told how, after a period of considerable struggle, she had finally made
the move out of an unhappy situation:

Barbara
*Q: You mentioned you had lived at this place for four years. Were you in a
group home before that?*
Ya.
Q: So you have been in a group home situation?
*I was in the worst one, I'll tell you that; it was just horrible. It was using us
for money. She took all of my cheques and used them for groceries and
everything. She had to get her licence taken away because there was a lot of
other stuff. She was going to go to court to get us back but I left and said no
way.*
Q: You put your foot down did you?
*Yes, because I went to see, there was four girls and we went to see the social
worker and we told them what was going on there.*
Q: You have to be able to speak out, don't you?
Ya.

Q: It is hard sometimes. We get frightened to say anything because we don't
know what is going to happen to us if we do speak out?
You know it was just like—after I left, it was kind of a feeling of guilt.
(Private, for-profit agency)

Barbara's experience suggested that while she was ultimately able to speak out, her sense of control over her life only went so far. Being supported by indirect individualized funding, she was not dependent upon any one service provider to meet her housing needs through a program-funded residential arrangement. But she had to gain sufficient strength to speak to the social worker who was ultimately responsible for overseeing her support and able to arrange for her to move from the unsatisfactory group home situation. Ironically, Barbara, perhaps as a result of being a very conscientious individual, felt discomfort at having taken this action. Nevertheless, the sense of relative freedom which was provided by the portability of her support dollars did mean that she could find an alternative housing situation in a family home where, as she reported to us, she was very happy.

Family Home and its Derivatives

In the family home arrangement, a person with a disability lives in the home of a family other than his or her own. Families receive payment or reimbursement for the support they provide to the individual. In some variations of the model, a family may accommodate several individuals. In principle, this model is an effort to support the development of natural family-like relationships between the "home provider" and the "home sharer." It is not conceived purely as a residential program, but rather as a means to support families to provide a home for an individual. The extent to which the model realizes its developmental potential in practice has much to do with the philosophy of practice of the families and agencies that offer it. While Barbara found her family home situation to be a considerable improvement over her former group home arrangement, in other family home situations that we visited, people often remained "clients" of the family home caregiver. For example, Susan, a family home provider, describes how Elizabeth came to live in her home:

Elizabeth and her family home caregiver, Susan
Q: Elizabeth, you were first taken to have a look at this place were you?
Elizabeth: Yeah, wasn't it Susan?
Susan: Well it was a little bit different. Usually that is the scenario but one of
the other gals that lived in my home has been a good friend of Elizabeth's for
many years, so it was sort of that kind of scenario. Pam lived there, so let's go

have a look up there. There was some changes done, we relicensed from four
to five clients and Elizabeth moved in with us.
Q: How did that happen?
Susan: Prior to Elizabeth living with me she had lived in a large group home
for about six months, and then she moved back home with her mother. And
mum being aged was looking for different avenues of what would happen down
the road and she asked me if I had room and we made room and we have
Elizabeth.
(Private, for-profit agency)

The Chance to Make Typical Housing Choices

Alternative living arrangements can provide a level of consumer control almost
unimaginable to people who know only the group home model. When people
labelled as developmentally challenged are able to make typical housing
choices and live as non-labelled people live, they tend to hope for and work
towards the levels of control and independence they see other citizens enjoying.
As well, when aspects of everyday life provide these individuals with greater
opportunity for self-determination in how, where, and with whom they live,
people around them may be more likely to be open to affirming and sharing
their aspirations.

One variation on the family home model involved an adult with a
disability sharing accommodation with a live-in caregiver and companion.
Here, the caregiver, typically a paid, full-time support person, was encouraged
to become less like staff and more a friend or companion. In such instances,
people had some autonomy in determining their living arrangements and in the
choice of fellow residents. One man, Ron, who had a live-in caregiver,
described how he and his caregiver, Phillip, were to be joined by a third
roommate in their rented home:

Ron
Q: Where you are living right now, is it a place that you decided you wanted
to live?
Yup.
Q: How did that come about?
Well, it was something that Phillip and I decided . . . that we were going to be
moving out of the other house.
Q: And the two of you decided you wanted to live in this house?
Yup.
Q: So is there anyone else you would like to live with or just you and Phillip?
There's going to be some other type of person that was going to be out of,
going to be moving out of [institution] and move in with Phillip and me.
Q: Is it someone you know?
Yup.

Q: And are you glad?
Yup, sure am.
(Private, for-profit agency)

Ron was not funded via a residential program, but instead received indirect individualized funding via a private, for-profit support agency. Being able to use his funding to purchase both his residential setting and support meant he was able to enjoy a level of self-determination beyond that available to many of the people living in group homes, whose housing needs were funded through the residential programs of the transfer agencies.

As we met with individuals with different funding arrangements, it gradually became apparent that individualized funding arrangements could create windows of opportunity for people. Of course, they needed to be aware of these individualized funding alternatives. But most importantly for those who were able to access such funding, they needed to be in contact with people who listened to them. Barbara's story ended happily because of the convergence of several factors. Funding arrangements provided for some flexibility. Although her housing provider was not an advocate on her behalf, Barbara eventually found one—a social worker. Barbara felt confident enough—empowered enough—to approach this advocate with her concerns and fears. Similarly, Ron had individualized alternatives to a group home and was fortunate in having connected with Phillip. Elizabeth, by contrast, played a more passive role in her move to an individualized arrangement.

Colin's story: purchasing a home. The people with whom we met who were supported by microboards were able to find housing arrangements that would have been inaccessible within traditional residential programs. These individuals were, of course, also receiving individualized funding and were not confined in the way a person would be within a residential program that was funded by program dollars. Among the more unusual housing arrangements that we saw involved the purchase of a home. Colin had been assisted by his parents in making the down payment. When he was growing up, Colin had lived at home with his family. We presented some of his story earlier in relation to his first attempt to move away from home into a group home. His parents explained how initially the only option available to them had been a group home. After that failed, and not without considerable struggle, they ultimately were able to find a far more satisfactory alternative. With the support and determination of his parents and other members of his microboard, Colin had relocated to a small home which he was purchasing:

Colin, with his parents, Cory and Henry
Q: So you mentioned when the group home thing collapsed, you started to think about this as an alternative situation. How did that happen?
Cory: It was attractive to us. Well, we started thinking about apartments first, although that was a very scary thing for us. We went around and we looked for apartments and we didn't find anything suitable.
Henry: Then Pierre, the facilitator, he works for the government, in the Ministry . . .
Cory: It was he that suggested why don't you look into a house, because we weren't having much luck finding a suitable apartment, or an apartment with a landlord that would allow us to make small changes necessary for a wheelchair. And so we shook our heads and said, "We don't know how ever this is going to happen, but we'll see what we can do." So first of all, our neighbour is a realtor, and he went round looking at houses and found this one.
Henry: Of all the ones we looked at this one seemed to click, convertible for accessibility.
Cory: Then we went to our friendly banker to see if it was possible for Colin to do this, what the mortgage might be, and how that would be looked after.
Henry: We thought we'd put it in his name, just in case anything happened to us; we had to do a few jumps there.
Cory: It's just possible to do this. We paid the down payment, Henry and I, and Colin pays his mortgage monthly from his GAINS [Guaranteed Annual Income Supplement].
(Microboard)

Colin had been in his home for two years when we met him. While his parents were closely involved in his life, they reported that they were now able to pursue activities outside of caring for Colin, whose disability was fairly complex and who would always need some physical support wherever he lived. His home was accessible, having been retrofitted to allow him to move around it in his wheelchair. He had 24-hour staff support, but did not require that overnight staff remain awake. The level of autonomy he enjoyed was clearly facilitated by having his own home and control over resources. For instance, he had choices around what his day and evening looked like, he was able to select his staff, and he was regarded as a neighbour and citizen of his community. The family was very clear about the impact Colin's living in his own home had made on their lives:

Colin, with his parents, Cory and Henry
Q: Could we talk about the question of different approaches to support and the impact of that on your lives, in terms of choice and control? Can you tell me what you think the situation is like for you—what about your sense of choice and control?
Cory: Well, at home, when he was at home we were tied down, pretty well, we didn't do a lot of things or he was with us when we did them. Like we couldn't go

golfing together. Then when he was in the group home, we had a lot more freedom . . .
Henry: That was with the respite care.
Cory: Yes, respite care, but there are things you'd like to do, but you were sort of losing control. I shouldn't say we lost, yes, I guess we lost control, not that we wanted to control Colin, but control what was happening around him. But now with this situation, yeah, if there's something you don't like, or you don't see, if there's opportunities you want to take advantage of, there's no problem, you don't have to go through a request list, or whatever, you just do it. And most of the ideas come from the staff too.
Henry: Right now, I feel that we are in control of what's happening with Colin. It feels like it's the best that it can be. I felt, when we were going through all that earlier, when he was going to enter the group home, I felt that we were included, but I certainly didn't feel like we were in control of anything. But then when it all fell apart, we were just totally out of control.
(Microboard)

It is interesting that in the context of life for adults with developmental disabilities, Colin's housing situation should strike one as being an innovative approach to securing a home. If he were not disabled, it would not seem innovative, especially in a culture such as Canada's, where the purchase of a home is a goal to which most people aspire. This fact alone speaks to the ongoing struggles faced by adults with developmental disabilities and their families in terms of having a secure future.

Josephine's story: building a home. Josephine, like Colin, was supported by a microboard. She was living in her parents' home when we met her but the hope was that she would shortly be able to move into her own place. The plan involved building a separate living unit for Josephine. Planning restrictions dictated that it not be free-standing, but rather annexed to the family house:

Josephine, with her mother, Melanie
Kent [Ministry facilitator] was just talking about a letter he had for me in the car. What we are doing is, we have contacted City Hall and we are setting something in motion. We are going to build, first we wanted to build it separate on our property but there's a lot of legality involved. . . . We sort of have set it for February, Josephine is officially to move out into her own home which is adjacent to her family home. And a lot of the reasons, and Kent promised us then we would have enough funding for twenty-four-hour staffing, that my husband and I are very much involved but it sort of would give, she is a young adult, it would give her the space to have a friend over and if she wants to watch movies until three o'clock in the morning that is her business. But it also gives my husband and myself our privacy back.
(Microboard)

Two major factors had helped bring a sense of liberation and control to this family: first, the availability of individualized funding for Josephine; and second, related to this, the formation of a microboard which was responsible for ensuring that she received appropriate care and support. In her mother's view, those around her had made the difference between Josephine being able to live a full life in the community and having to be cared for in a total-care facility:

> Josephine, with her mother, Melanie
> *Melanie: It has been, I must say the microboard has been really really good for Josephine. If she did not have a microboard, she would have been in an extended care facility by now. That is Josephine's only option is extended care . . . unless she had been institutionalized when she was small, she would then have returned to a group home situation and personally I wouldn't even like to see her in a group home situation; even though it is better than being institutionalized, still she wouldn't have the options that she is having now. She is also very fortunate because my husband and I, we have purchased the transportation for her. We bought our own van because without transportation you are nowhere. You need transportation. So my husband and I did purchase the van for her and the Ministry put all of the equipment on there that was needed. So it is a give and take situation. Like the same as building this dwelling for her. It will be my husband and I that will be footing the bill for the bricks and mortar, but they then will supply the staffing.*
> (Microboard)

Both Colin and Josephine had very complex disabilities and required fairly intensive support. They also had families that were financially willing and able to supplement the funding that was available through the provincial ministries. Of particular note, though, is the control and autonomy these families experienced under their present support arrangements. There were other examples of families who were very involved with their adult sons and daughters, and who also provided supplementary income to support them in their housing and other needs. However, they did not have anything like the level of control and autonomy that existed for Colin, Josephine, and their families.

Fostering Texture in Family and Home Life

In this chapter, we have chosen various examples of family and home life in an effort to explore those significant aspects of people's everyday lives. The housing arrangements we heard about differed from one another in several ways. Arrangements that people were happy with were also arrangements that made for more textured lives. Typically, these were more flexible and individualized than traditional, group home arrangements. They also looked more like typical North American living arrangements for people who do not have disabilities Most centrally, living arrangements that enhanced texture afforded individuals more control over where they lived, who they lived with, and how they lived. As well, people whose lives had texture typically had access to supports that were adaptable and able to innovate on an ongoing basis as situations changed. As people and families aged, and their needs changed, housing solutions that once made sense were no longer appropriate.

The experiences of the people we met with made it evident that where they live, or more specifically their homes, have important implications for texture in their lives. One simple but dramatic fact was evident in our discussions concerning housing. Individuals who lived within systems designed expressly to provide housing for people with disabilities talked about their homes in much more negative ways than did other people. There were often tensions when several unrelated adults were essentially *placed* into a home together, with little say about with whom they were to share their lives. The fact that many of these homes functioned at all is really a testimony to the people who lived and worked in them. It was especially when the philosophy guiding group home workers incorporated a commitment to personal control and individualized, responsive supports, that residents experienced a somewhat rich and rewarding home life.

Finding creative, unique solutions happened only when people around the individual with a disability had access to and were ready to act upon knowledge of what was possible. Colin's microboard, for instance, was faced with a crisis when his plans to move to a group home fell apart. They realized the possibility of buying a house only because Pierre, a Ministry facilitator, brought the idea to them. Pierre explained how this goal could be achieved, and neighbours and friends contributed in their unique areas of expertise. Colin's story illustrates how difficult it can be to carve out a unique housing arrangement. The family was forced by necessity to innovate and had to struggle against the system to make their idea work. Colin's solution was individualized and developed by those closest to him, but the microboard members had to learn as they went—no recipe was available for them to follow. Interestingly, the commitment and energy that Colin's microboard members invested in the process of buying a house paid off in a number of ways. The excitement and pride the group experienced when it became clear that buying a house was possible continued—microboard members were led to a new belief in their own capacities and experienced empowerment themselves through helping Colin to exert more control over his life.

This chapter allows some conclusions about the conditions under which adaptable, individualized, and person-directed housing arrangements were possible. Those individuals who had been able to find living situations that satisfied them, and that were more typical of those available to other people in our society, invariably had committed family members and friends. Living situations that involved smaller, more natural groupings of people than group homes—supported independent living, for example, or family homes—showed potential. However, they generally worked best when the individual had connections with people who shared a personal bond, a friendship, or kinship that afforded the individual the experience of unconditional acceptance and commitment. This is part of what most of us have in mind when we talk about a *home*—a place where we feel loved and secure, a place that brings warmth and texture to our lives.

A home in this normative sense is an empowering microcommunity, empowering for all of its members. If it is not to feel beleaguered and possibly wither, then the larger macrocommunity, mainstream life, within which it is situated, must be open to it. Not only must the facilities and services that the larger community offers be accessible to it; also the affective and productive relations that sustain the home as a home must reach out and connect the home with the mainstream.

Chapter 4

LIFE AND WORK

Adults with developmental disabilities seldom are presented with anything like the employment opportunities that those who are not disabled enjoy. Meaningful work, work in the mainstream employment market, and wages above a token level are all rare. A few individuals with development disabilities do have work that can truly be seen to enrich the texture of their lives. A small minority of the individuals we met had managed to secure a position for real wages in the regular employment market. Where people were paid, the amount of money they received was usually below what was otherwise recognized as minimum wage. Volunteer work was not uncommon. Often this volunteer work was in recreational settings, and the line between work and leisure pursuits became blurred. People sometimes weren't sure whether what they were doing was a job or a leisure activity. Nonetheless, volunteer work was generally regarded positively by the individuals we met. When people were not paid wages, or if they received payment in kind as opposed to a pay packet, they seemed less likely to have a sense of what it felt like to be in the role of a "worker."

The daily routines of most of the people we interviewed were made up of some combination of volunteer work and work at sheltered workshops or training centres. A considerable number of people continued to spend their entire days in life skills programs or in sheltered workshops. Compared to other aspects of their lives, people felt more comfortable expressing both dissatisfaction with their job and a desire to try something new. Nevertheless, just having a job, even if in a sheltered workshop, a setting into which few non-disabled people ventured, was often appreciated. Although the job isolated people from the wider community, it did enable people to sense that they were making a contribution. As well, it was the occasion for forming friendships and for interacting with one's friends. What we heard and learned about three basic types of work—sheltered settings, volunteer work, and mainstream employment—will be explored now.

Sheltered Workshops, Life Skills Programs, and Training Centres

Sheltered workshops are the most common form of vocational program for Canadians with developmental disabilities. Among the people with whom we met, the workshop experience was varied; some people actively sought out alternatives, including the pursuit of volunteer work to get beyond the sheltered workshop, while for others the workshop provided a secure and familiar place they identified with and where they found their friends.

Sheltered Workers Voice Satisfaction

A distinctive feature of the work situation for many who spent their days in sheltered employment situations was that their day-to-day activity brought them into contact with very few non-disabled people. Many lived and worked in a social world that involved primarily others with similar disabilities. This was not perceived as negative by many people. Barbara, who was actually involved in a number of different vocational activities, spent her days primarily with other people who were in segregated programs:

> Barbara
> *Q: So tell me about that, what is it that you are doing here?*
> *I am making cinnamon buns, and other things, like I help around cooking with various things that are in the kitchen, you know.*
> *Q: So this is like a little café here?*
> *Yes, we have people that are disabled and they come for lunch and they do exercises in there. Ya.*
> *Q: So you get some people who are disabled and some people who are not disabled coming here?*
> *Mostly disabled people that come in here and they come for lunch and they do their exercises.*
> *Q: I see. Do you come here everyday?*
> *No, every Monday.*
> *Q: Oh every Monday. And what do you do on the other days?*
> *I work at the [society].*
> *Q: Oh, what is that?*
> *That is a community workshop; it's a workshop for handicapped people.*
> *Q: So was it your decision to come here? How did that happen? What happened when you got this?*
> *I guess the social worker and house parents got me into this, so I really like it here. I like the people here, they are so friendly and nice and kind. . . . And I do volunteer work as well.*
> *Q: Oh, do you, and where do you volunteer?*

At [the pet shop]. I help them groom the dogs; you've got to help brush them, and wash them, and cut them, and clean their nails, and stuff like that.
Q: Tell me then how you feel about coming to this particular place to work. You say you like this? What is it that makes it special here?
The people you know, and to be talking to the girls, and to be with Lynn; we help her a lot when she is down and we help her out as much as we can.
Q: So this particular job you have here is a paid job, so you get a pay packet for this?
I get two dollars and fifty cents each week for coming here.
Q: Do you feel that that is enough? Do you feel you get paid enough?
Who cares.
(Private, for-profit agency)

Barbara seemed not unhappy in her various daytime activities. She appeared to gain a sense of accomplishment from being able to contribute in the work setting and from helping Lynn, who was the staff person responsible for running this vocational program. Most of their customers were persons with disabilities; very few members of the general public used the facility when the vocational program was taking place. Barbara had limited exposure to anything beyond these essentially segregated work situations. Like the vast majority of people, what mattered to Barbara was having a "job," regardless of the fact that it was within a sheltered workshop.

The workshop also provided friendships, served to anchor people's day-to-day existence, and provided a place with which they could identify and without which they could not imagine how they might spend their time or where they might go. Especially when they had had little or no opportunity to experience an alternative working environment, the workshop became an important focal point for a sense of community membership. With only less satisfactory workshops for comparison, some people were more likely perhaps to express satisfaction with their present situation. Jack spoke with conviction on behalf of others in his workshop when asked how he felt:

Jack
Q: In general is there anything you'd like to see different?
I'd like to see a bigger building.
Q: Why's that?
It's a bit too small for the amount of people that work in here. The law, the government, they're closing every one of the shops.
Q: What do you think of that?
I don't think it's right. You have so many friends here and you don't want to lose those friends, so why close the shop. I have so many friends in this job that some of them retired and they still hang around.
(Supported by public, non-profit agency)

Parents and Vocational Staff Often Set in Their Ways

In an effort to try to open up the world beyond the workshop to people working there, some staff incorporated programs designed to help individuals build towards more typical community experiences. One good example is the "muffin run" that both Norma and Esther participated in. Muffins were baked at the workshop, and the individuals, with the support of staff, took them to various offices and businesses throughout the community where they would sell them. People had an opportunity to meet a wider range of people and to make contacts in other workplaces that might lead to volunteer work or mainstream employment.

Unfortunately, few sheltered workshops take these kinds of measures to help their employees participate in community life or develop opportunities for other kinds of employment. The idea of moving into mainstream employment was not something people necessarily felt confident pursuing. For Esther, who was highly skilled but who had always worked in the sheltered workshop, staying at the workshop was important because it provided a sense of security. Her support worker, Paul, saw it this way:

> Paul, support worker to Esther
> *I think she works very well, she enjoys work. I think that any time I've been here visiting in the workshop she's always one of their better workers; she sticks with it. So I figure, I know they've been getting some of the jobs they do now out of here, certainly she could do some of them off-site. The difficult thing with her is that it will probably take a little time before she feels comfortable with it. Again, for twenty years work has meant coming to a workshop and not some different place. Again, the support staff are there and other people she knows are there.*
> (Public, non-profit agency)

In our interviews with some workers from workshops, we often heard them say that people remained in these settings because they did not have the requisite skills or behaviour to move out of sheltered employment. One staff member described her concern around people being able to move out of the day program she manages:

> Lynn, day program manager
> *I know I should make room for new and we are working on a system right now where we are bringing in new people and as long as I know that these folks are able to be here and I know that if I take them out on a Tuesday and that is their day. Then can you assure me that there would be ministry pride or whatever, that this person would have something to take its place type thing. It is difficult just to let go.*
> (Private, for-profit agency)

Clearly, whether or not people would aspire to and seek out alternative work depended to a considerable extent on the perspective of staff. The individual's future was often predetermined by the support worker's view of his or her potential—a view anchored in a "readiness" or "quality service" philosophy of practice. For the individual with a disability, a more empowering perspective would have been one that encouraged people to test themselves to find whether they did have the capacity to work in a more typical work setting alongside non-disabled peers.

Lori's situation makes the point. Lori was a young woman with some well-developed skills and competencies. She worked in a retail outlet within a sheltered workshop, but expressed dissatisfaction with that situation and a desire to move on. Evidently her view of the workshop differs from the view of her support worker. Comments from both people follow.

Lori
Q: So you are looking for a job then, what kinds of things do you want to do?
Work with dogs, work with kids, maybe being a secretary . . .
Q: So you're doing a bit of the job search, then you come here half of the day?
Yes, well, um, right now I am only seeing this lady one day a week and then the rest of the week I come all day . . .
Q: I see. So before you started the job search you worked at a daycare?
Yeah, volunteering.
Q: Volunteering? So you were working with kids there?
Yeah.
Q: So that's what you mean, about you would like to work with kids?
And plus I work at a daycare at church.
Q: So tell me about how you feel about coming to work here?
It's fun. Nothing else to do at home so I like to come here to work.
Q: Do you have friends here?
Yes.
Q: So you also work downstairs in the store? How do you like that?
Boring.
Q: Oh? Is it quiet?
Terribly quiet. On the weekends it's really boring.
Q: So that's why you are trying . . .?
Yes, trying to find another job, because I don't like to be bored, like to do stuff.
Q: You seem like a pretty energetic lady?
Yes, I'm very energetic, when I have energy.
Q: I wonder when all is said and done, would you say you feel pretty okay about things now?
Yep.
Q: What is your number one priority now?
Trying to find another job.

Q: So do you have any places in mind?
We have some places that [employment counsellor] was going to look at, different
daycares, vets, pet shops, and secretarial work, to see if there is anything suitable
for me.
(Supported by public, non-profit agency)

Lori's support worker, on the other hand, was quite a bit more tentative in her
comments regarding Lori's future. She obviously recognized Lori was a skilled
individual but was not open to sharing Lori's aspirations:

Donna, vocational support worker to Lori
It's hard to get her to work in the store now. There's not a lot to do and unless you
can kind of see the things that need to be done, then it's really difficult. When you
can't clean, I mean, that's a big part of doing the store, is doing that kind of stuff.
Q: So she can work the cash register?
Yes, her money skills are good. Sometimes she makes mistakes on change, but for
the most part she's good. She can use the VISA transactions. She'll call for
authorization.
Q: There's a lot of potential there?
Um, yes, for sure. She's a sitter though, that's the only thing. She does like to sit
so that you know as far as trying to train her to go out and work in the community
in a store it's difficult; she does like to sit.
(Public, non-profit agency)

Interestingly, on occasion, rather than seeing the job market as a problem
for people to break into, staff seemed to consider the person to be the problem for
wanting to work for regular wages in mainstream employment. While Judy felt the
sheltered workshop was a good fallback situation for people, she was also pretty
clear about wanting to get regular work. Her support staff seemed not to share a
recognition of her potential and it was likely that this served to inhibit Judy's
prospects for moving beyond the sheltered employment situation:

Donna, support worker to Judy
Q: Has work in the mainstream ever been an option for her?
Um, yeah, she up until recently she was doing pretty well, almost all of her work
was in the community. Volunteer work . . . so the problem with Judy is that she
always wants to find a paid job, and it's very difficult to find her a paid job. So one
of the things that we talked about or I talked about with [the director] is she does
so well on the contract work here that if we set up an enclave out in the community
that she could do that and hopefully we could work on them paying them piece-
work or a wage that would be more that the $0.43 an hour [that they get in the
workshop]. So she really seems to enjoy this work so and I think she'd like to do
something as well out of here.
(Public, non-profit agency)

Some family members expressed a desire not to have their relative engaged in work beyond the sheltered setting, and so in this sense, others' expectations tended to predetermine an individual's prospects, and people were simply not expected to progress beyond the sheltered workshop. In talking about her sister's situation, Jen was clearly not keen to see her sister involved in anything other than the vocational program in which she had been placed since leaving home:

> Jen, Geraldine's sister
> *Q: What about the workshop? What does she do?*
> *They do contracts there. She does very well at that. She's won the employee of the month three times. She likes what she's doing. They give them the work that they know they are capable of doing. I know that some of the others are going into the community to work.*
> *Q: Has that been an issue with Geraldine?*
> *No, I don't think she will ever have that ability to go into the community. I don't think she'll ever progress that much. That's what they are working for though, and I know that. It was quite a thing for them to leave home.*
> (Public, non profit agency)

Dissatisfaction Voiced About Workshops

Like group homes, sheltered workshops retain many of the features of an institutional setting. They are segregated. They tend to group people with similar needs. They are primarily organized and funded as programs, and as a result offer people relatively little choice or control over how they spend their time or whether they are able to work towards personal goals. Like group homes, they have been heavily criticized over the years. Some families were ready to spell out their dissatisfaction in relation to the day-to-day experiences of their family member in the workshop:

> Remy, Belinda's mother
> *My idea of her days, she gets up in the morning, has a bath, breakfast, then goes off to the workshop or whatever you want to call it. I'm not as happy with the workshop as I am with the home. The ratio of staff-to-person isn't great. They have too many people to look after. I guess I want Belinda to have individualized attention all the time, but I'm a mother. I feel the workshop is probably a waste of time. I don't feel she is getting much there, other than she has to have somewhere to go in the day. They do well with what they have, but it isn't what she should have.*
> (Public, non-profit agency)

Another family member explained what he saw happening in workshops as people aged. His concern related to the limitations of viewing the sheltered workshop as a lifelong pursuit:

Rich, Julie's brother:
*They are finding that as women reach around 45 that they tend to be less interested
in the workshop settings and are having to review their program. They are finding
that they would rather have less work and more recreation. They are finding more
with females than with males, so there has been someone hooked up with Julie to
look at more recreation options.*
(Public, non-profit agency)

There was indeed evidence that as people aged, the idea of attending the workshop
simply didn't appeal to them and they had made a very clear determination about
how they would spend their days:

Beatrice, with Janine, support staff
Q: You're retired?
Beatrice: Yeah.
*Janine: She volunteers at the Y, it's part of her day program. She puts towels in
the washer, folds them.*
Beatrice: I'm going Tuesday.
Q: Why did you decide to retire?
Beatrice: No more at workshop, no more [sheltered workshop].
Q: You didn't like it?
Beatrice: No, no more.
Q: Why?
Beatrice: It was bad.
Janine: She didn't like it.
(Public, non-profit agency)

Value in Volunteering

For several people like Beatrice, whether they were a young adult or a more mature
person who might be thinking of retirement, unpaid work or volunteering provided
an attractive alternative to being in a sheltered workshop setting. From people's
accounts of their experiences, volunteering often provided them the opportunity to
make a contribution or to know that they could make a difference. Julie's
experience demonstrated this. Her volunteer job involved cleaning at a nursing
home. However, she made sure that while she was working around the home, she
managed to connect with the residents. Her brother, Rich, explained:

Rich, Julie's brother
*She was doing some volunteer work. She tended to socialize with the patients
rather than simply work. So the patients had some bonds with her. She worked in*

a seniors' residence as well. It was social interaction and they gave her recognition. They had birthdays and teas and they recognized her with a dinner. (Public, non-profit agency)

A number of the volunteer jobs were based in more social or recreation settings. This may suggest that the line between work life and leisure became blurred, but generally for the people we spoke with, the integration of these spheres of life was not problematic, and often it was the sense of being able to be a contributing member of some group that made the difference. Ron had a volunteer job at a fairly major recreation centre where several of his peers were placed as part of a job experience program:

Ron with Max, agency staff
Q. Do you have a job at the moment?
Ron: Yes, doing the [recreation centre] one.
Q. Doing what?
Ron: Volunteering stuff. Like doing mirrors, steps and all sorts of other stuff, yup, yup.
Q: Very good. Do you get paid for that?
Ron: No. I get free food.
Q: Good. How much can you eat? Is it worth it?
Ron: No, it's not a thing. I just get it for nothing any time I work there.
Max: He gets to use the facility as well.
Ron: I get to go into the gym and have a workout and stuff like that. I just have to get my arms and chest here, and here, and here and my leg built.
Q: So you do some body building?
Ron: Yup, Right.
Q: Would you like to have a job?
Ron: Oh yes.
Q: What would you like to do?
Ron: Oh, handing out coins to all the people at [video game store at the mall] and hand them the coins and they hand their money over to me, and I hand them the coins to play the games with. And that stuff.
Q: Is that an amusement park?
Ron: It's just full of games and stuff and food and drinks and stuff.
(Private, for-profit agency)

Bev was another person who did custodial work at the same recreation facility as Ron, and like Ron, she received free admission to the facility as payment in kind. It was significant that the trade-off for Bev in giving up the volunteer job would be the loss of a leisure pursuit that was clearly meaningful to her.

Bev, with live-in caregiver, Judy
Q: Where do you work?
Judy: Where do you work?
Bev: At [recreation centre].
Q: What do you do there?
Judy: Bev, she wants you to tell her about your job. You clean drains. She does
cleaning there. What do you do?
Bev: Cleaning and, clean and, cleaning the bathrooms.
Judy: Good.
Q: Is there something else that she does?
Judy. Depending on the season, like right now because it's so busy with summer
programs and stuff she does the towels, the laundry there. And then in the
afternoon, like at one o'clock, she gets to do the weight room. She goes and works
out and then she gets to swim for the rest of the afternoon, which is her favourite
thing to do is swimming. . . . She has been working there for about four years. One
day a week, only, and it's Mondays. And we were thinking of taking her off that,
by the request of her last day worker, but Bev really did express on her own how
important that place was to her because she loved her swimming and had she
missed it then she wouldn't have had that to look forward to.
(Private, for-profit agency)

The use of people to perform tasks for payment in kind obviously raises questions of equity, and at times dignity, for the person. But the issue of whether or not the experience is valued by the individual is perhaps the most critical point. Clearly, these opportunities provided people with alternatives to going to a sheltered workshop and they often helped to open up pathways to the community for people. Joe's experience was a case in point:

Joe, with mother, Freida, and father, Klaus
Q: Do you work some other place too?
Joe: Yes at [golf course]. Look here on my shirt.
Q: That's a lovely golf shirt. Did they give you that?
Joe: Yes, for free.
Q: Do you golf there?
Joe: Yup, for free. And they give me free food down there.
Q: And what do you do to earn the free food and the golfing?
I can't do both. Play golfing and the food.
Q: You can't do it at the same time?
No.
Q: No, I hope not.
Freida: But what kind of work do you do?
Joe: Pick up balls.
Q: Is that all you do there?
Joe: Oh ya. Tuesday mornings I work at [nursing home]. And there is another
job. I am working deliver flyers.

Q: I heard that you do flyers. So you are a busy guy?
Joe: Oh ya.
Q: Is there anything else that you work at?
Joe: On Wednesday's something at [golf course].
Klaus: I think he cleans the clubs as well.
Joe: Yup.
Q: Do people pay you when you clean their clubs?
No.
Q: Is it the rental clubs?
Freida: No, it's private. They store the clubs at the club and when they are stored they are always cleaned.
(Private, for-profit agency)

The more rewarding volunteer experiences certainly appeared to be those where people were engaged in something that was intrinsically engaging, challenging, or stimulating, rather than simply providing a means to an end by keeping people busy doing relatively menial tasks that no one else was interested in taking on. As well, as Fred explained in relation to Nick's involvement with the Society for the Prevention of Cruelty to Animals, where he cares for strays and cleans cages at the animal shelter, the recognition that a person receives as a volunteer reinforces the sense of worth and value the person has for the organization:

Fred, live-in caregiver to Nick
Nick likes to work and he's very focussed on what he works at, and when he works at the SPCA, twice a week and he loves it there and the people love him. And he was chosen, he was the only person chosen as a matter of fact, to go to the volunteer festival where all the volunteers in [the city] came and were given a stage show and a dinner and so on. He was chosen for that.
Q: Did he go through the orientation?
No, he didn't have to because he already had work experience there. They knew him there. And right now he is one of the best workers there. When Nick works, he works. He is very focussed on his job. He does not take breaks, he does not fool around.
(Private, for-profit agency)

Because the opportunities for people to pursue typical employment situations were so limited, people used volunteer opportunities whenever possible to help bring a sense of purpose and worth to their daily situations. In doing this, some people spent part of their day in a workshop setting, and did what they could in the community as volunteer opportunities presented themselves. The sheltered workshop continued to be perceived as important though, because it was an environment where people knew they had a place, so to speak, and would not be turned away because of lack of skills or ability. Judy received minimal financial remuneration of $0.43 an hour for working in the workshop, but she knew it was a place where she could feel that she was making a contribution, as she says, "help out."

> Judy
> *Q: You work here and elsewhere?*
> *I do a little bit of volunteer work at [the home].*
> *Q: That's a nursing home?*
> *Yes, it's on Fox Glen. And then I'm in here part time and I come in if they need some contract work done and I help in the store downstairs if they need some help.*
> *Q: So in terms of the workshop, if the workshop wasn't here at all would it be difficult for you to find other things to do with your time?*
> *Yeah. A lot of the places won't hire you because you don't have your education. Here people can come in to help out. You can come off the street and help out.*
> (Supported by public, non-profit agency)

Mainstream Paid Employment

Very, very few people we met had managed to secure a job in the mainstream employment sector, and not surprisingly, those who had, found the fact of having a job and receiving remuneration a source of great pride. Chad was one of those few. He reported on his success in gaining a job that paid him a small wage:

> Chad, with his support worker, Doug
> *Q: Your mother was telling me that you work. Is it at a warehouse?*
> *Chad: Well, yes.*
> *Q: Can you tell me a little bit about what it is like there?*
> *Doug: What is the name of the place?*
> *Chad: Be-Seen Signs.*
> *Q: And you do some painting on the signs?*
> *Chad: Well, ya.*
> *Q: That sounds interesting. Do they pay you?*
> *Chad: Yes, twenty bucks every Friday.*
> *Q: And you get that money yourself?*
> *Chad: I get that money from Al [the boss].*
> *Q: Is that important to you?*
> *Chad: Yes, I think so.*
> *Q: How did you find this job, Chad?*
> *Chad: Well, I just find out. I just went over there and check it out.*
> *Q: Did somebody go with you?*
> *Chad: No. I just went there by myself.*
> *Q: What do you like about it?*
> *Chad: That's a good place.*
> (Private, for-profit agency)

Having secured a position in the competitive labour force did not mean that people were subsequently regarded as fully autonomous in relation to managing their affairs. Betsy was able to get a real job that paid real wages but she continued to have relatively limited independence around the management of her affairs. Her mother explained:

Susan, Betsy's mother
She works at [the hospital]. She's been there for sixteen years now. She works in the kitchen. She gets as much wage as you or I would, so she makes close to $11/hr.
Q: How did she get this job?
She was just fortunate. She was in the workshop. She went to the manager and said get me a job. The first person didn't want to walk up the hill to get to work. Then Betsy was the second person he had in mind. So it was a six-month basis. After a week Betsy's boss called and said they wanted to hire her and if you don't let me hire her then I'm gonna find someone else. So now, she gives the paycheque to [her worker]. She gets $50/month out of her pay [for spending]. She will never get any more. She made in excess of $20,000.
(Public, non-profit agency)

As for people's chances of advancing and gaining greater control over their work life in mainstream employment, it was not unusual to hear expressions of really quite low expectations from both family members and staff. Support staff indicated the difficulties they faced in pursuing employment opportunities for individuals. Many of those difficulties obviously resulted from systemic barriers to the hiring of persons with disabilities in mainstream employment. The experience of continually confronting those barriers appeared to shape the perspective of some staff in such a way that they held few aspirations or hopes for the individual's future. This was not a universal response, however, and when invited to dream about a "best possible scenario" for the individual, a lot of staff were not hesitant to suggest exciting and interesting alternatives:

Stephanie, support worker to Jane
Q: So is she a likely candidate for more community employment in the future?
If things come up that she is interested in possibly, possibly. She is pretty good at reading; like she said, she goes over and reads to the kids. Her reading is not too bad, her writing is a bit jumbly. As far as typing or something like that, like with computers she is really, really slow so something like that I don't think unless she gets to be quicker at it. As far as reading at the library or something to children or at the school, I could see something like that; working at stocking shelves and that, it's a possibility if she'd like to do that. Um, she's never brought that up. She likes working with the kids I know that, with children.
Q: In her planning sessions, is it the case that you would be able to suggest the possibility?

If I felt that the opening was out there. Like we do have some people contact us that need someone, like the vet to clean the cages or something. If there is someone down there that we think would like to do that we can suggest that and we have done that with a few of our people and it works out great.
Q: If you had a dream for Jane's future what would it be?
Myself and the way Jane is? I'd like to see her working at the school more, not just reading, maybe being a teacher's helper. Two days a week is fine, and they just think they are great over there.
(Public, non-profit agency).

What was most disappointing, though, was the realization of just how infrequently these sorts of dreams were fulfilled. But exciting things did happen for people beyond the more traditional approaches to working life, and it was evident that with determination and creative thinking on the part of the individuals we met and those around them, people sometimes found ways of making what might have once seemed impossible become a reality.

Beyond Work: The Possibilities of Individualized Approaches

Given the challenges of breaking into the employment market, to continue to push forward and assist people to move beyond the workshop required considerable commitment and energy from support staff. Staff sometimes had no option but to find creative alternatives because people simply did not find the workshop a comfortable place to be. Oftentimes, it was funding regulations and limitations which prevented people from moving beyond the workshop, because the dollars required to support them during the day were attached to vocational or day programs within the workshop. But every now and again, people were able to seek and develop alternatives, with the support of those close to them. Beatrice's story is one example. Beatrice's support staff were able to help her get out of an unsatisfactory situation and still receive the support she needed. They did this through innovative approaches to funding, which allowed her to have support outside the workshop:

Marg, support worker to Beatrice
Q: Can you give me a sense of her day there? What's the routine?
One of the things that happened, the previous supervisor knew Beatrice didn't like the workshop, she acted up on the bus. They did everything they could to accommodate her. She just was unhappy there. So one girl said why don't we take her out of there and put someone in that really wants to go. So she drew up this program and the city bought this program from 9:30-2:30 at home. This morning she's volunteering at the Y and I guess that is going well. They love Beatrice.
(Public, non-profit agency).

For another individual, Tanya, significant efforts had to be made to find an alternative to the workshop. Once identified, that alternative provided an environment in which Tanya flourished:

Crystal, support worker to Tanya
It was impossible that, you can't even get in the door with her. So I decided that it would be much better with my personal experience that I would try it, and it was just way off kilter. Tanya could not even accept the odour, and the noise level was extreme, which for Tanya was difficult; because she has no sight, her other senses exhilarate, which is fantastic for us. So we decided we would have to find something else. There's a unity centre, a spiritual based. We gently brought her in for two or three minutes at a time and we would use potpourri as a stimulant, we would let her feel that and she would panic and she would go. Tanya now makes sachets, it's her own business. It's not anything to do with a government subsidized program or anything. She graduated to plastic hearts, filling baby food jars, and wall plaques that are decorated and filled. The unity centre is going to expand this program to include three other visually impaired people and they will then share the profit. Mother is very, very pleased and helps as much as she can. Tanya goes to the unity centre every morning. There's about fifteen different items that she can accomplish now. She's doing very well there. There's at least an average of $80/month that she brings in. If she was in a workshop that would be the fee. She goes four mornings a week, so her recreation is also her work.
(Public, non-profit agency)

The more flexible the funding arrangements, the more individualized and generally more appropriate it seemed support services could be. When we spoke about work with individuals whose support services were the most highly individualized in our study—that is, those people supported by individualized funding and the microboard model—we heard stories that were strikingly different from those of people served by traditional organizations. Traditional jobs or vocational placements had proven difficult for some microboard users in the past. It was clear that with individualized funding, flexibility, and the ability to be creative in planning, the way in which their days were organized had much more to do with individual choice as opposed to what was available in terms of programs and staff resources for a group of people sharing a similar disability. When funding accompanied the individual, the range of options was greater. Clara, whose son was severely disabled and who was supported by a small microboard, commented on her son's day:

Clara with her son, Richard
Q: In a day, what happens in an average day?
He accesses adult education at a local college. It is a literacy program for people who haven't finished high school. It is open to anybody, any adult who wants to learn either English or math, basic English, basic math. And Richard started that

last year because he wanted to continue his education. . . . Yes, so he goes to the adult education program where I am not quite sure he is doing what he likes because right now he's talking about pulling out. And there is nobody specially trained [at the college]; there is an aide but we usually send one of the caregivers along with him because we thought it would be better, but it puts of lot of weight on their shoulders. That's what he does; and then he goes swimming twice a week. He's really into physical activities. He goes to the gym twice a week. He loves to bake and we didn't want him to eat all this stuff so we said, what can you do with all the stuff and we found a food bank, a shelter near here. So they take a bucket full of stuff over there, they give us the ingredients now; so he bakes, takes it over. He loves it and he does it any time he has the chance.
(Microboard)

Similar choice and self-determination were available to Josephine, who was supported by individualized funding managed by a microboard. Josephine had complex disabilities, including being non-verbal. Here, Jean, her support worker, explains what a typical day was like:

Josephine, with her support worker, Jean, and mother, Melanie
Q: Are you also doing day activities with Josephine? Tell me the sorts of things that you are involved in.
Josephine goes to college twice a week and she takes communication courses and I help Josephine out; she communicates by her pictures. So we do that in class with her other companions that go to the class too.
Q: This is like a community college?
Yes, and then we usually go for coffee and we meet her friends that are finishing classes at the same time and we go for coffee or drinks up at the cafeteria. And Josephine just got a dog recently, a very loveable, loveable thing. And Josephine takes Sook to all the elderly homes in town and we have a lot of people that we know and we have conversations with, and we tell them about our lives and stuff and we bring Sook up there because they are not allowed dogs any more in the homes. And so we bring Josephine's dog up there. He just loves to get all the attention. And Josephine goes swimming twice a week and she can swim. We both together, although I get tuckered more than Josephine does. We swim about twenty laps of the pool each time and then we go have some fun time. Josephine has learned to love the hot tub, so we have to hit the hot tub. Not no more though 'cause mum and dad bought Jo a nice hot tub. . . . And she has her physio that she does every day. Josephine has an adult tricycle which she has her dog on the front of her bike that pulls the trike and her and I go for our rides around the block. And she has got her walker and she does her exercises on her walker. And she has a couple of foot exercises that we try and do every day. And then there is just a lot of what Josephine enjoys doing. We make sure that along with the daily things that sort of need to be done, that Josephine still gets everything that she would like to do in her own time. Josephine watches a lot of her movies in her spare time that she just loves. She has a galore of all her favourite things to do at home that she

does all the time. We make sure that we don't take that stuff away from her, she enjoys it so much. She has a pool in her backyard that she swims in. In between that, she's on trips here and there.
Melanie: Music, too.
Jean: Oh yes, and she does music therapy once a week but we are probably upping that to twice. We talked about this year when Josephine goes and plays on her instruments. She has her instruments and everything that she works on and everything. And the music teacher's working with her.
(Microboard)

As we heard from people in traditional support situations—that is, people outside of a microboard support system—there was a certain security and certainty of the sheltered environment that was hard to contemplate losing. This fear was shared by families whose relative was receiving more individualized support, but it seemed that once that initial hurdle had been overcome, people enjoyed the opportunity to try new things. Colin's mother explained:

Cory, Colin's mother
It was a real concern, to give that up, because after he left school he was going there [to the workshop] every day and he loved it, but on the other hand, actually, Pierre from the Ministry encouraged us to give that up for a while to see what we thought. I was really reluctant, but he is just a spectator [at the workshop]. I mean, going there every day and being in the same environment every day, all day long, so Pierre said, would we consider that, and we did and I think it's worked out better for Colin. He gets around; he's taken more into the community.
(Microboard)

These stories describe rich and varied daily routines. The same was apparently true for others whose support allowed a high degree of control over how they spent their time. Their aspirations were listened to, affirmed, and acted upon by those around them. Here were potent illustrations of the power of a person-centred and capacity-oriented philosophy of support. However, each story was a description of a unique individualized solution that made sense in a specific set of circumstances.

Fostering Texture in Day-to-Day Work Life

Reflections on what people with disabilities do on a day-to-day basis have highlighted another critical component of a textured life. Most of us look to our working lives to provide us with a sense of achievement, of having made a contribution. This opportunity to give rather than receive was obviously important to the people with whom we met as well. However, it is difficult to share of yourself when those around you see you as having little to offer. Among the adults with developmental disabilities that we spoke with, the hallmark of a rich and rewarding vocational life was a network of support that validated the individual's capacities, hopes, and dreams.

Interestingly, people who appeared hesitant to complain about less than ideal living situations often expressed an interest in pursuing something different in their day-to-day work lives. When people were happy with their working lives, it was often true that their workers recognized their capacities and shared their desire to do well. Workers who did not believe an individual was capable of anything more than sheltered work rarely provided that individual with opportunities to try an alternative.

Volunteer work was one avenue that people pursued, often with the support of staff. Volunteer jobs differed from sheltered work in several important ways. They tended to bring people into more integrated social settings, where they met a wider variety of people. As a result, volunteers had an opportunity to make a contribution to the larger community through their work, and to be recognized for doing so. Volunteer settings tended to be more individualized and varied than the opportunities available within workshop settings. Furthermore, the individualization of volunteer work made it more flexible and adaptable: the potential to move on to new activities over time, and even to access mainstream paid employment, seemed greater for those who were in volunteer jobs than was the case for those who worked only in sheltered settings. While volunteer jobs could confine people to more menial tasks than people might typically pursue in the community, many were viewed as more stimulating and rewarding alternatives to the workshop. People who volunteered in the community typically had more say in where they went and how they spent their day than those whose only vocational experiences were in workshops. There was fairly clear evidence from what people told us that volunteer work can provide an opportunity to further develop capabilities and give people a chance to know they are making a valuable contribution.

When funding arrangements were sufficiently flexible to enable people to develop creative, individualized work situations, such as starting up a small business, developing one's artistic gifts through working at home, or attending college or school, the experiences were clearly more natural and liberating for people. This flexibility meant that people were able to have support in their home or in the community, as required. As suggested in the case of the people supported by traditional organizations, when funding accompanied programs rather than individuals, people were more likely to be attending sheltered workshops or life skills programs. This is the inevitable result when dollars are directed to agencies to run vocational programs. The determination of what is available is then made by the agency. Unless the individual is financially independent, he or she lacks the means of seeking out alternatives to the workshops and life skills programs which the agency puts in place. While these arrangements may have provided a secure environment for people, they rarely functioned in ways that brought people into the community beyond. Instead, they enclosed people in a "world of disability."

Chapter 5

LIFE, LEISURE, AND RELATIONSHIPS

Social relationships are a part of normal everyday life. These relationships comprise a central part of our social support, which in turn relates to our sense of well-being and an understanding of who we are. This aspect of life underlies much of what we have said thus far. Now it becomes a central focus. At first glance, improving the living and working conditions of people with developmental disabilities may seem best served by enhancing the tangible resources an individual can access. Such resources are, of course, indispensable. But richness is especially brought to the texture of our lives when we have healthy, respectful, rewarding and mutually empowering relationships with other people. The more we talked with people, the more evident it became that understanding texture in the lives of people with developmental disabilities first and foremost requires understanding how these individuals, and the people that are important to them, conceptualize and communicate the nature of their relationships with one another. Our study provided us with rich and thought-provoking evidence that the social construction of relationships had profound implications for the texture in people's lives.

Social interaction occurs in most things we do on a daily basis, at work, at home, and in the context of our leisure time. Through this social interaction we establish and maintain friendships. If our data are any indication, one very old and problematic way of looking at relationships and friendships of people with disabilities still survives: some people continue to believe that friendships are not as important for individuals with developmental disabilities as they are for other citizens. Or the view may be that although the individual may have a desire for friendships, the expectation that the desire might be fulfilled is not realistic. We were able to learn from the individuals with whom we met what they considered desirable and realistic and what mattered to them about their social relationships. Their friendships varied, from relationships in the community at large, to close and intimate relationships with other people with developmental disabilities, and for some, caring and committed relationships with people who were paid to support them. Hence, we were able to gain a deeper understanding of the meaning of social relations and how they influenced the texture of people's lives.

Segregated Social Relations

We have indicated that generally people spent most of their time, at work and in other settings, with other individuals who also have disabilities. Since the vast majority of their involvements occur in segregated groupings, it should not be surprising that most of their relationships were with individuals with disabilities. As we explain in the final chapter, the tendency has been to devalue such relationships. Devaluing these relationships suggests one more way that others have traditionally defined what is good and what is appropriate for this population, denying them autonomy and self-determination.

Easier for Staffing

One reason people seemed to spend so much of their free time with the people with whom they lived and worked is explained by the availability of staffing resources. If they lived in homes with several others, and their main opportunity to get out of the house in pursuit of some recreational activity depended on staff being able to accompany them, then it was likely that they would go out in a group, supported by one or two staff. One mother talked about her daughter's activities. It was evident that her social relations and social interaction were essentially confined to the people she lived and worked with and the people who provided support in the home:

> Kathleen, Eileen's mother
> *Sometimes they do things individually, but on the weekends sometimes the two staff will take them out together to do an activity together. If one wants to do something the other staff is here with the others. They have Special Olympic bowling. She likes the socializing. People from the workshop go.*
> (Public, non-profit agency)

Indeed, many of the people we met were involved in segregated leisure activities, like bowling; that was where they congregated with their friends, who were also part of the support services system. Margaret's response to who her friends were and where she had met them was fairly typical:

> Margaret, with her live-in caregiver, Onalee
> *Q: Who are your friends, Margaret?*
> *Margaret: Mandy and Cindy.*
> *Q: How do you know them?*
> *Margaret: I know them from bowling league.*
> *Onalee: Do you have any other friends Margaret?*

Margaret: Diane. Same bowling as I go.
Q: How did you meet them?
In the bowling alley.
(Private, for-profit agency)

So it was that the organized nature of people's free time and social lives meant that typically they were moved around the community in groups made up exclusively of individuals who had a disability and congregated with others who were participating in the same program-based activities. Staff worked within the program structure to ensure people had a chance to socialize in their free time:

Stephanie, support worker to Jane
Q: The bowling? Is that out of here?
It's run through the group homes but almost everyone here [in the workshop] goes to it. It starts up again in September and it goes all through the winter and I think closes off about June. They close down and they do repairs or whatever, but uhm, but most of our guys go Friday nights, that's their Friday night thing. They all go bowling and they have their little snack and their drink, and they have their bowling game. It's another activity that they all get together at, it's a night out.
Q: In terms of other sport, would anything be able to happen there?
Actually, I have papers on my desk for a baseball team that I have to hand out today for all of our guys.
Q: Is this new?
No, well, actually new this year yeah. They tried it last year but it didn't seem to work out so good. They're going to do it again this year. Like there's level one, level two, so they sent me the sheets yesterday and I'm gonna hand them out today. People signing up so there will be a baseball thing going on in the summer and as far as the swimming, we do have a swimming. We do have swimming on Wednesday nights but we have a Special Olympics on the Monday night too . . . the Olympic thing . . . it was on the same night. We had the Special Olympics and then our swimming was on the [same] night so we tried to discuss with them, could they put the Olympics swimming on another night so that they had the option to have both if they wanted, which they did this year, having the Olympics on Monday and our's on Wednesday. So we worked that out because a lot of our ladies and gentlemen like Special Olympics but they also like our class as well, so now they can have the chance to go to both.
(Public, non-profit agency)

In most cases, it was simply assumed that people who lived together would vacation together:

Ginger, support worker to Belinda
Q: What about your roommates, do you like them?
She gets along well with them too. She's the outgoing one.
Q: What does the group do together?

They go to parades together. Walks to the park, go the Dairy Queen.
Q: Do people at the workshop do things together after work?
They socialize at work, but [the workshop] has an appreciation dance once a year.
And there are also dances at the community centre at town that you see a lot of the
people she works with. So they do get together, about ten times a year outside
work.
Q: What about the weekends?
We went to a vacation for four days. We get away once a year for a nice vacation.
We went to a farm.
Q: What are you doing this year?
We haven't decided yet what we are going to do this year. . . . One of our residents
isn't feeling too well, we'd like her to come so we're trying to delay it as long as
possible.
(Public, non-profit agency)

Often this was a matter of financial necessity—travelling together to a
segregated camp, for instance, was one way to overcome transportation barriers
and ensure that everyone got a vacation:

Eli, support worker to Jack
They do take a vacation. They do go to a camp; they do fund raising. We like to
do day trips that don't cost anything if we can do that. We know what it's like for
these guys that don't have anywhere to go. Generally it's transportation that is the
problem. Places to go but no way to get there. Next Wednesday we are going to
charter a boat and he's going on that one. We have a hayride, but Jack won't go
on that because of getting him on the wagon would be difficult. And we try to go
places where they want to go.
(Public, non-profit agency)

Also, opportunities to socialize with other group home residents from
within the same agency happened fairly routinely. Esther's support worker, Paul,
described some of the involvements that cut across the agency:

Paul, support worker to Esther
There are a lot of activities that usually go on, that she participates in some and
some she doesn't. She enjoys going out for supper, visiting friends at the other
homes quite frequently. Some other activities like baseball, there's the bowling
they do, things like that she has participated in. And she has as well some
friendships with some of the people that she knows from working [at the
workshop], from some of the other houses that she goes down to.
(Public, non-profit agency)

Social gatherings organized by agency staff that brought people together from several group homes provided occasions for involvements with family members as well:

> Crystal, support worker to Tanya
> *We have a lot of interhouse activity. You have a supervisor who has three houses so that the houses get together for parties or barbeques, so we would have nine residents here and we would have quite a party, so that there's a lot of socializing. There's at least two barbeques a year, house parties; so parents are encouraged to be involved also.*
> (Public, non-profit agency)

Finding Reciprocal Relationships

As we have suggested, many people's lives kept them essentially cocooned within the world of a service system. However, it is equally important to note that close relationships with housemates or co-workers within the developmental services system were frequently the most solid and truly reciprocal connections people had within social networks that were otherwise fragile. Judy provided an illustration of how important these connections could be. She describes how Bev, who had tended only to see staff as her friends, had befriended another young woman who had lived in the same home for a while:

> Judy, Bev's live-in caregiver
> *She always says, you know, "Bev and Judy are friends." I mean, Bev loves the socializing, she loves socializing and she'll sit here all day and say, "We're all friends." So it's important, friendship has just recently become important, and I think it's because we had a temporary person live with us and she got very used to having another person in the house that was younger than her and she got to be the older sister. And so it was quite fun for her. And they are now continuing their relationship.*
> *Q: Oh, that's good. Is it a disabled person?*
> *Yes, she's autistic. This is the girl going away with us. She lived with us as a temporary emergency case. And she moved in with my girlfriend who is also a caregiver and we live a mile apart.*
> *Q: So they can see each other quite often?*
> *They go to and from work together every day. So they've got that kind of communication.*
> (Private, for-profit agency)

In another situation, staff had facilitated the development of close bonds between two fairly severely disabled young women who lived in the same group home. One of these women, Tanya, generally tended to shy away from any contact beyond the worker she knew very well. With support she gradually responded to her housemate, Megan, and they had developed a warm and trusting friendship:

> Crystal, support worker to Tanya
> *We have a gal with Rhetts syndrome, and at first Tanya would not let anyone near her. I used Megan to motivate Tanya into the living room because she would not of course leave the kitchen, and I used Megan to motivate her. She would of course come with me and hang on to me as she does now and then Megan would be introduced and she'd touch Megan. It got to the point where she would move right into Megan and they'd snuggle and verbalize to each other to their own sounds. There's sort of a purring Tanya does when she's quietly content, and she would do that with Megan. Then we would have little dances in the living room, so that's how we got Tanya to relax in the living room. This is your home so that's how we got Tanya to relax in the living room.*
> (Public, non-profit agency)

A number of people spoke of the value they placed on longtime friendships they had with peers who were also labelled developmentally disabled. Christine describes two relationships, one with a man she grew up with and another with a man that she met in a sheltered workshop:

> Christine
> *Q: Where did you grow up?*
> *Got a friend I grew up with.*
> *Q: Have you, who is that?*
> *A guy.*
> *Q: So where did you meet him?*
> *He doesn't live far from where I do, no he doesn't. . . . I also have a good friend named David. He is a really good friend for a long time.*
> *Q: When did you meet David?*
> *I have known him since 1984.*
> *Q: That's a long time.*
> *A long time.*
> *Q: Where did you meet him?*
> *At a workshop, that's where I met David, a long time ago, that is where I met him.*
> (Supported by private, for-profit agency)

Wanting Intimate Relationships

The fact that adults with developmental disabilities seek normal intimate, adult relationships has tended to be ignored or denied by people around them, by staff, and by family members. But it was quite typical for the adults with whom we met to wish for the same sort of meaningful relationships with other people that are enjoyed by other adults. Barbara, one of the individuals we met, talked candidly about the perception held by the general population concerning the relationships people with disabilities should be able to have:

Barbara
Well, people in wheelchairs, I think there could be more houses where people that have a disability, like they should have houses where disabled people can get married and live, and be in the phonebook like other couples. I think it would be good you know, but I don't know if they will allow people to get married.
(Supported by private, for-profit agency)

One of the challenges for adults with developmental disabilities is that any relationships they seek tend to take place in an environment that feels like a fishbowl. Comments on Ron's friendships indicated how his social life comprised primarily activities involving other adults with developmental disabilities. These involvements were seen as warranting careful scrutiny by staff:

Bill, support worker to Ron
Q: His friends are predominantly the people who work with him on a regular basis. Would he have a chance to meet some young women or to have a girlfriend?
Oh, absolutely. They have dances for mentally challenged people or wherever, you can take him to different places to meet people.
Q: So he may meet someone and have a friendship of this nature?
Oh yes, and then again you have AIDS involved and you've got having a baby involved; so there is responsibility that again he's got to handle as well. That's where the worker has to step in to a certain degree to help them with those certain things.
Q: Has he ever told you he was attracted to a woman?
Oh yes, he likes women. He's even brought Playboy magazine over and I told him I'm not interested in that. We're at work and stuff. But it shows that he is definitely interested.
(Private, for-profit agency)

Some people we met were not prepared to comply with the expectation that they would not be involved in a normal adult relationship. One such couple was Jack and Norma. Describing their situation, one empathetic staff person noted:

Eli, support worker to Jack
Jack has a lady friend, and for a long time he has wanted to move in with her. Jack has some health problems. Where he is living now they can't.
Q: You mentioned his lady friend?
His fiancée, actually he's given her a diamond.

Q: Any realistic hope?
*I think it is. Her family don't like him. But I think it's more that they see her
having to take care of him. And she is developmentally handicapped as well, so of
course, we're talking about older parents, they're in their eighties and they're
really worried about what's going to happen to my daughter when I'm no longer
around. Plus the fact that if she has to take care of him too, uhm. When I was her
support staff we used to work around a lot of things but then I moved from
residential to vocational, so I don't have the contact any more, but I used to. But
we did work out a lot of things, and I don't think her family is quite as opposed as
what they were, but I think if anything does come of it, it will be when her family
are no longer around.*
*Q: That's a tough one, people don't think of this with adults with developmental
disabilities?*
*People don't ever stop to think that they have a life as well. I mean they're not any
different than you and me. They have the same feelings.*
Q: The same need for human contact?
Yeah, but parents somehow see their children as being sexless.
Q: Especially with the older families?
*Yeah, it's not so bad with the younger ones, but the older parents, I mean sex just
was never in that vocabulary at all.*
(Public, non profit agency)

Jack and Norma, meanwhile, were prepared to do whatever it took to maintain
their relationship. Jack explained the situation as he saw it:

Jack
Q: So how about friends that you know in this area?
Oh, I'm engaged to be married.
Q: Who to?
Norma Price. We've had some problems with her mom and dad, but we don't now.
Q: No more problems?
No.
Q: So you bought Norma an engagement ring?
Yeah.
Q: She's a nice lady. We met Norma.
Yeah. Norma. I started going with her six years ago in June.
(Supported by public, non-profit agency)

Norma still felt some concern around her parents' knowing about the relationship:

Norma
I have a boyfriend. I have a ring.
Q: Is this an engagement ring?
Yes it is.
Q: So does that mean you are planning for the future?

Yeah, but I don't want my family to know.
(Supported by public, non-profit agency)

Despite the barriers, this couple were undaunted in their commitment to each other and it was evident that they were not prepared to give up on the dream of ultimately being able to marry. They spent as much time together as they could, and worked at being able to do the sort of things couples typically do, as Jack suggested:

Jack
The girlfriend and I, we try to go over to [the park]. The last long weekend that we had, we went over there and had a picnic. We plan our weekends.
(Supported by public, non-profit agency)

The apartment building that Norma lived in was not wheelchair accessible and in order for Jack, who used a wheelchair, to get into the building, they had to seek help. Friday evenings was their time to get together at Norma's apartment and routinely they were assisted by a group of bikers who frequented a local coffee shop close by Norma's apartment. These men walked with them over to her building and then lifted Jack and his wheelchair up a few steps so that the couple could have that time together in her home. While Jack and Norma's story is certainly inspiring, it gives a vivid illustration of what might normally be viewed as insurmountable barriers to the development of a lasting relationship. But this couple had a community of people around them who supported them in ways that gave them back at least some control over their lives, so that they could continue to live as other ordinary citizens who choose to engage in caring relationships.

Howard, the man whose comment opens this book, had once had a relationship with a woman he still talked about. Flora, his support worker, felt the end of this relationship had left a huge void in Howard's life:

Flora, support worker to Howard
Q: Is there anything that you think he might want to change?
The one thing he does talk about is his old girlfriend. When he did move down here he lost contact. So I am assuming she doesn't know where he is to contact. He said they were very close and he refers to her as his girlfriend. I know he would probably like to see her. I think he would probably like to have a girlfriend and more friends.
(Public, non profit agency)

Howard's situation was not atypical. He told of the relationship that he now considered lost forever:

Howard
Q: Is there anything you would like in your future down the road?
I don't know yet. I'll tell you what happened once. This girl that I knew in school,
she's handicapped, she takes convulsion. We tried to get married, our parents
stopped.
Q: So you didn't get married?
Not to her. She was my steady girlfriend.
Q: So you've had a few girlfriends?
Yeah.
Q: But no steady girlfriend now?
No, are you kidding? I doubt if I'll see her again. Right now I could kiss her
goodbye.
Q: So that's history, eh?
Yeah that's history to me.
Q: She moved away?
As far as I know she lives in [town] with her parents.
(Supported by public, non-profit agency)

Steve talked about caring for Esther whom he had met through a sheltered
workshop they had once attended together. He had managed to maintain a periodic
relationship with Esther and told us that he looked forward to seeing her during the
annual holiday, which took place at a camp for people with disabilities.

Steve
Q: So what about holidays, do you get to take holidays?
Once in a while we go some place with residence.
Q: Are you going somewhere this year you think?
I don't know whether they're planning to go or not and Esther Weber is the one
that likes being with me a lot.
Q: Is she your worker?
No, she's my little girl.
Q: Your friend?
Yes, she's at 121 Greenview.
Q: Is that a residence?
Yeah. She just stays there all the time in her room and her and I use to be at the
time, when I use to be at ARC here she enjoyed being with me a lot. Mimmie use
to hit her once in a while and I use to guard her and made her stay off of Esther,
she would run right straight for me, she would put her arm right around my neck,
and I just guard and made them stay off of her.
(Supported by public, non-profit agency)

Many adults with developmental disabilities do not have continuity of
relationships in their lives. Relationships are disrupted by factors largely beyond
their control, resulting in further isolation. It seems almost paradoxical that parents
who had committed much of their lives to providing support to their son or

daughter occasionally found it difficult to step back and allow the individual to explore life and more typical adult relationships beyond the family circle. Good intentions were sometimes misdirected as a result of assumptions about the kinds of relationships that were possible or acceptable for people.

Seeking Social Relationships in the Community-at-Large

While some people clearly had rewarding relationships with other labelled individuals, it was also evident that many of the people we spoke with were not happy with a social network that included only people with disabilities. As important as relationships with other labelled people can be, for some the desire to meet people beyond the service system was strong:

Claude
Q: Where are some of the places you go?
Swimming at l'Ouest house. Restaurants with people from here.
Q: How do you get there?
By foot, bus or the minivan from here.
Q: Do you meet friends at these places?
Not really. I have a few friends but. . . . I see them when I swim.
Q: Do you have a good time with these friends?
[No response.]
Q: Is there something you would like to do in your free time but can't?
Going out more, with people not from [this agency].
(Supported by public, non profit agency)

Significant social relationships can and do develop with individuals outside the human service system. Some of the individuals we met made a deliberate choice to pursue relationships with others in the community. Whether or not that happened depended to some degree on whether there were mechanisms in place to facilitate establishing and maintaining the relationships.

Just as volunteer work is something that becomes part of the everyday experience of many adults with developmental disabilities, so too does the concept of a volunteer friend who can connect a person with the community at large. The following observations from a support worker, Donna, illustrate the way in which people come to accept the idea of volunteer friendship as not only desirable, but almost essential to an individual's well-being:

Donna, support worker to Lori
Q: With her friendships, she talked about Amy, can you tell us about that?
Amy was working here in the workshop with us. She was a student and she was
hired on. I think that Lori and her got talking and realized that they had common

interests, and I mentioned to Amy that Lori was looking for a volunteer buddy. She did have a volunteer buddy who had moved and couldn't spend the time with Lori so they just kind of basically took it upon themselves to call each other and they took it from there, which is quite nice.
Q: Lori mentioned that she suggested it, that she made a phone call?
Yeah, she took the initiative to do it, which is wonderful. Because I think Lori has a difficult time with friendships. So she has in the past, and some of the things that her mom said when I first started working with Lori, some of the things that she would like Lori to have is a volunteer buddy that is similar, you know in interest to her and close to her age so that could have some time with her because she finds she is just spending too much time with her, that is her mom, and she didn't feel that was really healthy.
(Public, non-profit agency)

Keith, who indicated how difficult it was to find friends, reinforced the view that volunteer friends have an important role to play:

Keith
Q: So do you think there is somewhere else you'd rather live?
I don't know. I am trying to get girls to know me, and it's hard for me to get a blind friend that I know. I used to work for the CNIB . . . another thing is that I get along with my volunteer, Damon. He takes me swimming on Mondays, and also I play piano.
Q: So Damon is a volunteer friend?
Yeah.
(Supported by public, non-profit agency)

Other people also had made a conscious effort to move beyond the service system and connect with people in everyday settings in the community. This obviously took courage, particularly when people were essentially ignored by others in those settings and remained on the edge of the social group, as was the case for Lori when she joined a fitness club in her town:

Donna, Lori's support worker
She also goes to aerobics. She joined it herself and goes there on her own, usually three nights a week. It's right on the main street, it's co-ed, which is very good. She is very dedicated to going, far more than I am. But as far as making friends, I haven't heard much about that. So I think she kind of goes, does her workout and then leaves.
(Public, non-profit agency)

Mary Ellen, a woman who had a hearing impairment, had reached out and had been successful in making friends with her neighbour. Here was a relationship based in reciprocity and mutual respect, something that was not always available to people:

Mary Ellen, with Marg, support worker/interpreter
Q: Do you have any friends around here?
Marg: Neighbours, I met a neighbour of yours the other day, Gladys. Is it Gladys? The lady that you watered her plants. Gladys, over there, your neighbour?
Mary Ellen: Did you talk to her?
Marg: Yeah, do you remember when I met her, you took me to meet her.
Mary Ellen: Yeah, we, she has helped me an awful lot.
Marg: She said that you helped her too.
Mary Ellen: We've been friendly, it gets pretty lonely in here by myself. She knows that too because she is alone. So we go and have a cup of tea and that, being friendly. I do my crocheting and she does her knitting.
Marg: Gladys said that Mary Ellen was very good to her. She said that Mary Ellen took care of her when she had her cataract operation. Mary Ellen was coming in and watering her flowers.
Mary Ellen: Yeah, I watered her flowers, her plants for her.
(Private, for-profit agency)

These contrasting experiences indicated to us just how complex individuals and their relationships are. Most especially, though, it seemed to point to the importance of ensuring that people have the option of associating with those who share tastes, preferences, and interests. At the same time, those choices need to be facilitated and supported. In a closed system that won't happen. As well, it has been argued that people paid to be part of a labelled individual's life can never, by definition, function as true friends. We would argue otherwise. Based on what we learned from the people with whom we met, genuine friendships can and do develop with people who are paid to provide support. We'll see examples of that later in this chapter. However, not infrequently staff members themselves may express in subtle ways that they do not see the people they are paid to support as equals or as true friends. In addition, agencies may place limits on the kinds of relationships staff can form.

Facilitating or Blocking Pathways to Community:
The Role of Staff

A long standing debate in service provision focusses on the role of paid support in terms of facilitating relationships between persons with disabilities and other community members. The worry has been that staff can act as a barrier to the formation of natural relationships. Among the people we met, staff were generally more concerned about keeping people occupied, and this often resulted in a busy schedule out of which natural relationships rarely emerged. This is not to say, however, that staff were not cognizant of the importance of facilitating social interaction and friendships, as suggested by Tina's comments:

> Tina, Bonnie's support worker
> *And that's what's good about our art classes because with Artists Unlimited it's for many different people with different disabilities, and there's a lot of people there. So basically what we do when we go to Artists Unlimited, on coffee break, I like it because it is a very social time. So you know you are in a big classroom and you are working, and then you have a coffee break and Bonnie and I go and sit with all different kinds of people. The staff is in there and the craftsmen. But from time to time I will go sit somewhere else and I will kind of watch Bonnie in the crowd and there are times when she sits at a table with a bunch of people but she is not initiating conversation with anybody. She actually is in her own little world, talking to herself. Sometimes I may come over and say, "That person sitting next to you, you know her, that's Susan, why don't you say hi, how are you." And she will if she wants to, and if she doesn't want to she won't. And that's fine. But I just try to remind her that you can say hello to people. You don't need to have a huge conversation but just a "hello" is friendly.*
> (Private, non-profit agency)

Since Artists Unlimited was a segregated leisure program, any friendships that the worker might have facilitated here for Bonnie would have been with other individuals with disabilities.

Another individual, Elizabeth, was supported by a worker, James, who was paid specifically to link her to new leisure activities. The involvement with James had introduced her to some leisure opportunities in the community, but it was not evident that they would lead to a more integrated life in the community as a whole. Elizabeth continued to spend her spare time with other disabled persons. The people she lived and worked with, or who were paid to be with her, comprised her social network.

> Elizabeth, with her caregiver, Susan
> *Elizabeth: Well, last weekend we went swimming at the new pool, that was kind of nice.*
> *Q: The two of you?*
> *Elizabeth: Yes, there were lots of people there too.*
> *Q: Is this a place that you have been previously, to the pool?*
> *Elizabeth: I think it's about the second time that I've been over there, right Susan? Unless it's the first time, I can't remember.*
> *Susan: James hasn't taken you swimming before has he?*
> *Elizabeth: No.*

Susan: He sort of makes a Wednesday plan, for the following weekend and they do different activities. They've had in-home video rentals and they've gone to the movies.
Q: Did you go to minigolf at all?
Elizabeth: No.
Susan: It's basically a very casual, social program. I believe he has three clients that he takes with him but all of them don't come all of the time. Very, very, very casual.
(Private, for non-profit agency)

Other support staff saw it as important to assist people to break out from the immediate one-to-one interactions between staff worker and the people they support, by facilitating connections with other people in the community. This takes skill and commitment from the staff person. But few realize that this sort of facilitation would make a significant contribution to the person they are being paid to support. Marg was an exception. She supported Mary Ellen, the woman who talked about her friendship with her neighbour. Mary Ellen, an extremely talented artist, had been trying, with Marg's assistance, to gain access to a local art and crafts group. The staff there had indicated that, because Mary Ellen was deaf, without an attendant to support her she would not be able to join the art group:

Mary Ellen, with her support worker, Marg
Q: They say she has to have somebody with her?
Right, Mary Ellen, as you can see, lip-reads extremely well and you would never know that she is completely deaf, if you weren't told or until you had a conversation with her for a while and realized that she wasn't hearing everything. But in a group where more complicated instructions might be given, things need to be written down and therefore the people there say that she needs someone with her to write the instructions down . . . so that is something that I have to work on, to go there and find out exactly what those classes are like, find out; who knows, maybe there is a peer there who would love to write things down for her, in which case she has created a buddy or whatever, a friend, an advocate, support who is also a peer. That may not be there, so I have to, I want to make sure that whatever support she gets, that it is solid. Because this is her life, her art, her ceramics. This is her life.
(Private, non-profit agency)

   Where there was sufficient flexibility in the way support was funded and organized it appeared that staff were in a stronger position to facilitate connections and relationships between the person they were supporting and the community. This was most evident in the case of the microboard approach to support where there was room for spontaneity in people's everyday activities; the individualized nature of the support allowed for greater self-determination and freedom in how the person related to the community. Jean explained how she was able to accommodate Josephine's interests, in the process of which Josephine became far more visible in the community, and enjoyed greater opportunity for social relationships outside her immediate circle of support:

> Jean, support person/companion to Josephine
> *Josephine travels, she loves going for walks along the dykes, loves her walks, the harbour quay, the mall, she loves going to the mall, just being out constantly. Josephine is not a homebody, a person that likes to stay at home. She is usually up before us in the mornings and stuff, wanting to go out. In the summer it is very busy because Josephine is not very well in the winter usually and she usually has to be indoors to keep her health so it is not fun for her in the winter. But when summer hits, it is usually from May, June, we try, to October.*
> (Microboard)

For most other people, however, the pattern was fairly predictable. Few encounters with the world beyond the service system happened in their lives and hence the prospect of finding a pathway to the community was diminished. A lot depended on staff being able to realize the potential people had for connecting with other people, making friends, and ensuring that opportunities for breaking out of a world of social isolation were there. As Clarke, who was an owner/manager of one support agency pointed out, independent living did not mean people could simply be placed in an apartment and then have it be assumed that they'd naturally connect with others in that community setting:

> Clarke, agency management
> *They are in a funny little nether world. They know they have issues and they have money management problems, hygiene problems, socially isolated or socially inappropriate in that they might go to bars to find friendships or whatever. So that is our challenge is to try and recruit them into more appropriate community leisure activities. But they are supposedly, I guess, the crème de la crème. They are the people that have sort of achieved independent living and yet it's a little shortsighted to isolate them in their little apartment and they want to do a little job, but they have no friends.*
> (Private, for-profit agency)

For this agency, as well as others, working to connect people socially was something the workers believed to be part of good practice. Where the challenge lay was often in having the energy and commitment to have that happen.

Some staff saw their role as linking individuals with others who might become true friends. The difference was in how they thought about their relationships with the people they served. Recognizing the importance of human relationships, they often played an active role in trying to enrich the lives of people through friendship development. Keith's support worker Sandy was a good example:

Sandy, support worker to Keith
Sandy: I know he really wants to have a girlfriend. Telling him about different things he may have to sacrifice to have a relationship, or things they might have to do. Lori [client] has become a friend to him. I have always stressed that to Keith. We want to fade out of being staff. Keith is very good at that, he looks at us as friends. He is also good at making volunteer friends.
Q: So how does that work?
A few years ago I requested volunteer support. So I put in a referral to Zanna for a volunteer friend for Keith, to take him swimming and coffee. Damon wanted to go swimming, and so did Keith, and that is how they were connected. They look at the volunteer interest and match it, or sometimes they come in to the workshop.
Q: So Damon has been involved for a few years?
Yeah, and Keith is beginning to have consistency.
Q: You've talked about relationships, where do you start when you are facilitating that?
Keith, when he first started was depressed and withdrawn. He has come out of his shell. He speaks now. Those he feels more comfortable with and those who he didn't. He has said he wants a girlfriend and girls involved. So we just talk to him about it to ask him what kind of relationship he wants—someone to go out for coffee with, or to go for walks with? What does it mean to him? What do relationships mean to him? It is all done in conversations, an everyday chit-chat. What we have tried to do is when he said he wanted to have a girl to have dinner with we would ask him who he wanted to go to dinner with and he will ask, and assist him to take them to dinner.
Q: So has this happened yet?
Yes, he has gone to dinner a couple of times, and she is interested in him as a friend. He goes in spurts where he does and doesn't want it. We don't encourage it or discourage it, we leave it up to Keith.
(Public, non profit agency)

As in this instance, then, workers were clearly in a position to play an important role in the process of helping people to develop friendships both within the social service system and in the broader community. It seemed that generally few staff were actually ready to take on that role, however. People with developmental disabilities were often grateful for any form of social interaction that approximated friendship. And so, often, they came to view volunteers and staff as friends. For their part, most staff in traditional human service settings did not see the relationship the same way. As we shall in our discussion of "placeholder" relationships, in many instances relationships with staff were characterized by superficiality and an absence of genuine respect and reciprocity.

Placeholder Relationships

Not infrequently, the relationships people with disabilities had with their support workers were very important to them. The worker was often someone they spent a lot of time with and got to know quite well. These relationships were often complex. The attitudes or philosophy guiding the worker made a profound difference to the nature of the relationship they formed with labelled individuals. This helps explain why there is concern when people's only friendships are with staff. The power imbalance between the individual and the staff person can increase the vulnerability of the individual.

These are placeholder relationships. During the working day, staff and volunteers may spend social time with people. Labelled people often are very grateful for the attention, but these interactions differ from true friendships in many ways. The power dynamic is extremely unbalanced, and the potential for dependency is high. The stake that one participant holds in the relationship is far greater than that of the other.

At a private, for-profit agency that served people who were primarily supported through individualized funding, a senior manager indicated that her agency shied away from encouraging relationships between staff and the people they supported:

> Deb, senior staff
> *Q: In terms of your staff, what is your feeling on friendships and so on between the people who are paid to provide support and those supported?*
> *You're going to like the people you're going to work with, they are good people, you are going to establish relationships with them; I don't agree with people taking others home. It is against our policy to do respite, caring for the people in your home that you are supporting. If you choose to stay in contact with somebody once you are no longer involved with them on your time, then that is your choice, but I don't agree with making promises that you are not willing to keep, and I make that very clear. It's human services. We really can't expect not to establish relationships, but the boundaries still need to be there. You are just a worker, you are not the saviour or the last word.*
> (Private, for-profit agency)

While an agency may discourage friendships with staff, a dilemma presents itself when people essentially have so few chances at developing natural relationships and friendships, that they grasp at the chance to be friends with their worker. George, who receives support from James, an employee of the above private, for-profit agency, talked about how he saw his relationship with James:

George, with his mother, Bernice
George: It's going really well between me and James. We're kind of like brothers, you know, like kind of like a big brothers kind of thing. Someone to take me out if my mom can't take me anywhere, helps me out, and I learn quite a bit from him and he learns some from me. And he gets information about me and I get information about him. When I first met him, I was first shy because I didn't know who he was but my mom says he's kind of cute but . . . (laughter) it's going really well.
Q: What kind of things is he going to be helping you with?
George: He's going to help me feel confident about things. He's going to help me, me and my mom in general, me, mom, to get into more activities and stuff too. And he's told me that he's single, he doesn't have a girlfriend, so he's a single man like me so that's another thing we have in common, me and James have in common we're both single. This is the first time that I've ever had a true friend that actually stayed with me, well not stayed, but like took me out all of the time.
(Supported by private, for-profit agency)

The bothersome fact about this is that George seemed not to know that James would actually never be his friend, partly because it was counter to the agency's philosophy, and partly because of the way he felt about George. James's perspective provided us with some insight into why people ought to be concerned about the power imbalances between the worker and the individual. His comments here are patronizing and certainly not reflective of the way real friends would talk about each other:

James, support worker to George
You know, he's not quite there 100% but you're not really sure what it is about him, other than maybe you think he's just a bit geeky. If you didn't know that he was diagnosed a certain way, you might just think he's a bit of a geek. Other than that he seems normal. He's a nice guy, he really is. But he's small and a little too attached to his mom. I like working with him because I can talk to him, and in this field that's the hardest part for me is working with people that I can't communicate with clearly. I really like the verbal interaction, and with George I can do that quite well. And it's fun. We can joke around and talk. But then with people who are non-verbal, that's where I have my most difficult times.
(Private, for-profit agency)

The lack of consistency and commitment of support that people experienced was exacerbated by the fact that staff were often not permanent features of their lives, and while relationships may have been established, these were often relatively short-lived. The relationship may have ended for the staff person who left, but the person to whom support had been provided likely held on to the memory of that relationship and struggled with the fact that the person was no longer part of his or her life. Ron's comments illustrated this most clearly:

Ron
Q: So Phillip is a good friend of yours and it sounds like Melissa is too. Who are your other friends who you like to do things with?
There's my mother and some other people that I know.
Q: Do you see your mother very often?
She comes to visit me every now and then.
Q: When we were outside this room you mentioned the fellow who was in the picture out there?
That was my worker. The one that I miss a lot.
Q: It was a worker?
Yes. I miss him still.
Q: Where did you meet him?
He used to live with his mother and I used to live at his home, where him and his mother lived.
Q: You lived at their house?
No, no. I went to visit them. I worked with, I'm his best friend. But we both worked together. I always go to his house and I come in and him and I come in and we always have lunch and we watch TV and we end up having peanuts to eat too. Q: You will have to get in touch with him sometime?
But now him and his girlfriend are living together all in one apartment at the Fairway Centre. And where all the other stores are.
Q: Maybe you could meet them for coffee one day?
Yes, I could phone. If I phoned I could get a hold of him and let him know that I was wanting to come and see him. And him and I could have a talk about what things us guys would want to do. It's just that I can't seem to stop picturing him in my mind.
Q: Is there anything else you would like to do in your free time or any other people you would like to be with?
It's hard for me to think of people that I seem to miss a lot.
(Supported by private, for-profit agency)

Given the fragile and weak social networks that people had, it was not surprising then that the loss of a staff member whom an individual considered to be a friend often had a devastating impact on the individual when so much was invested in the relationship. Beatrice's mother noted the way in which the departure of a worker had been personalized by Beatrice, who somehow blamed herself for the worker leaving:

Margaret, Beatrice's mother
Q: Does she like the staff?
Oh yes. One of the problems that might have triggered this depression, they left. One of them wanted to go and do something else, go to a different place. Beatrice still talks about her. One staff is a live-in, and Beatrice became close to her. Strangely enough is that she had depression and was hospitalized. Beatrice has

always been close to the staff, and sometimes she thinks it's her fault, I've been bad and they left.
(Public, non-profit agency)

Mutuality and Moving Beyond the Worker/Friend Distinction

Throughout this book, we have used the experiences of people served through microboards to explore what happens when the process of providing support to people with developmental disabilities is completely removed from the traditional agency system. Within microboards, we saw fundamentally different kinds of relationships between staff and the people receiving support. In this context, the traditional dichotomy between worker and friend begins to break down, and new kinds of relationships without power imbalances seem possible.

In the microboard situation, people appeared to have more individualized or personal relationships with their staff. However, the relationship between Josephine and one of the people who was paid to support her, Jean, was so strong that it moved into an entirely different realm. For instance, Jean, a paid support person, was better described as a companion to Josephine, rather than her worker:

Josephine, with support person/companion Jean, and mother, Melanie
Q: Would you call yourself a key worker or full-time worker?
Jean: Yeah, I guess.
Melanie: We actually like to say companion.
Jean: Yeah, I like that word, if that's okay . . . [for instance] if we go to the beach or something the other workers usually follow along and we just all go as friends, we invite all of Josephine's friends and we all go in groups and just do everything together. We don't really see it that way.
(Microboard)

Here was a genuine friendship between an individual and the person paid to support her. The way in which Jean became Josephine's companion is significant. The following paragraphs tell their story:

Josephine, Jean, and Melanie
Q: Did you go to the same school?
Jean: No, I met Josephine at the summer rec program one year. It's a cute story.
Melanie: It is a cute story if I may interrupt here. About six years ago Josephine went to the summer recreation program through the Association for Community Living, and so the first day when I picked Josephine up, Jean came bouncing down the stairs and told me that she was Josephine's key worker for the summer and she introduced herself and all that. So I said, "Oh yes, that's nice"; so I got into my car and I pulled off and I said to myself, "Oh yeah that bouncy little thing—three days and that is the end of that." So I was really surprised by the end of two months, when the summer program was over and I picked Josephine up at the final

day. Jean came over and bounced again down the stairs and asked me if it was okay. She said she had never worked before with a person with disabilities but she had had so much fun with working with Josephine and would it be okay if she could be Josephine's friend and come to the house and do things with her or whatever.
Jean: And I took her to Aqua Friends and we did the swimming.
Melanie: And that's when I said to Jean, okay you want to be her friend, how about taking her every Friday from 3:30-4:30 to Aqua Friends, which is a swimming program at Aqua Centre. She said yes, she would do that. So she did that for a full year. She would take Josephine swimming, and by that time the At Home program kicked in, and so that's when Jean became our, and I personally don't see Jean as a staff person either, she has been more like a daughter. She travels with us on holidays and my husband, Josephine, and myself, she does all the medical appointments and everything and we are quite comfortable sharing one home together, just like family.
How do you feel about that?
Jean: Yeah, that's the same, yeah.
(Microboard)

Josephine and those around her experienced mutually reinforcing strength and growth within the microboard setting. Important to note, however, is that having a microboard and receiving individualized funding does not make this sort of balance automatic. When microboards first emerge, they may take time and care to nurture. In their formative stages, they may encounter challenges to their development and initially little may happen among the members. Clara recounts the difficulties she and her son Richard experienced in finding a comfortable balance in terms of staff relationships and the provision of appropriate support when Richard first received funding and they started the formation of a microboard:

Richard's mother, Clara
Q. Have you had to terminate people?
Oh yeah, we had to do that last year. We weren't very good at recruiting because we didn't know what exactly he needed. And we were nervous and we thought he needed friends for him, or that we needed to make it like a family. That kind of turned out to be very difficult because sometimes people invited him over to their place and did all sorts of strange things. But the work didn't get done here and then people were saying, well, I took you over to my place. We keep it much more professional now, we say this is what needs to be done, if you want to be friends fine but you can't exchange it for the work. We are doing it much different now and yet it works what we did. I think that he was really emotionally abused by a couple of caregivers. Last year I changed things and we don't have anybody full time. We have a rotation of four-hour shifts because I feel that the togetherness, you know if you don't have specific tasks to do you just sit here and talk and philosophize, you know, talk about religion and all sorts of things. There is a real danger for that to happen in settings like that because there is no supervisor, there

opportunities for textured lives by helping people make connections in the broader community. They helped to open up what is often a very closed developmental services community, and allow freer movement to and from other spheres of community life.

What is affirmed by this is that reciprocity and community are important aspects of everyday life. Social relationships are a principal source of people's empowerment-in- community. One thinks here of Josephine's success in entering the wider community. Of Mary Ellen's friendship with her neighbour. Of Jack and Norma's, and Steve and Esther's, relationships. Of Tanya's friendship with Megan. Among the factors that influenced people's experiences was whether or not opportunities for relationship development were recognized and acted upon. When this happened, people were more likely to experience a true civic identity and a feeling of connectedness to community.

Chapter 6

A SOCIAL ECOLOGICAL THEORY OF EMPOWERMENT

As we noted in chapter 1, empowerment is regarded as an important social goal by researchers in a wide range of fields. We also mentioned there that in an effort to better understand empowerment, much of the research in the human service field, including health, social work, and social psychology, has focussed on individual experiences and outcomes (cf. Bradley, Ashbaugh & Blaney, 1994; Dunst, Trivette, Starnes, Hamby & Gordon, 1993; Hayden & Abery, 1994; Kuyek & Labonte, 1995; Lord, 1991; Lord & Hutchison, 1993; Ozer & Bandura, 1990; Wallerstein, 1993). Other researchers, notably in fields such as community psychology, community development, and planning, have examined empowerment in the context of the collective or community (cf. Christenson, Fendley, & Robinson, 1989; Florin & Wandersman, 1990; Friedman, 1992; Zimmerman, Israel, Schulz, & Checkoway, 1992). Under the rubric of "social capital," Putnam (1996) has identified community-level capacities such as civic engagement as critical elements in the development of empowered communities. Empowerment is about "becoming" and is a process that is never really complete (Raphael, Brown, Renwick & Rootman, 1998). Along with others (e.g., Rioux, Bach, & Crawford, 1997), we have linked individual self-determination for people with disabilities to human rights policies, a commitment to democratization, and an atmosphere of mutual respect and equality.

There appears to be consensus among these various researchers that empowerment is a dynamic and multi-dimensional concept and that it is associated with at least three main characteristics. First, it involves a change in individual and/or collective capacity, which in turn influences control. Second, empowerment can be experienced as both a process and an outcome. Third, a necessary condition of empowerment is interaction between the person, the community, and the social and political spheres in which the person exists.

According to much of the research, the social and political spheres typically bring the individual into some sort of power relationship with others as he or she struggles for control over resources. It has been suggested that in order for people to experience empowerment, they first need to gain control over resources, so that a social relationship of dominance emerges, with one person gaining the exclusive power to act on the resources. Hence, on this account, the inevitable outcome is that within the social relationship one person controls resources which the others covet (Serrano-Garcia, 1994).

Our findings supplement but importantly modify this earlier research. What we have learned is that empowerment is tied to the social context in much more profound ways than is often imagined. When the individuals with whom we spoke experienced empowerment, there was not simply a shift in where decision-making power lay. There was a shift in thinking and in the character of relationships, where the focus was on relations of community. Here the process and the outcome are what we have identified as empowerment-in-community, as manifested by a textured life.

Theory Building

The results of this study suggest a social ecological theory of empowerment, wherein empowerment is understood holistically in the social context in which the person is embedded. This context, which provides the individual's life with *texture*, forms as it were, an ecosystem. Analogous to the balance and symbiosis found in natural ecosystems, the process and outcome of empowerment are *mutually reinforcing* among the people who interact with one another in that social context. This means that empowerment is much more dependent upon a balance of power among the interacting individuals than is suggested by conceptualizations which portray empowerment as resting on domination. In the social ecological perspective, then, empowerment is not something that occurs in isolation, outside the social context, and beyond social relationships. One person becoming empowered does not require that others become proportionately disempowered; in fact, people's life experiences appear most empowering where there is an equitable distribution and sharing of power. Empowerment depends on a synergy or balance among those who are in the social relationship. The symbiotic nature of the relationship is characterized by respect and reciprocity. So it is that as one person in the relationship gains a sense of accomplishment and growth, of flourishing, those around that person flourish as well.

In situations where people flourished, we noticed they treated one another differently. Authentic friendships were more common. Distinctions between paid support and friends seemed less sharp and less important. Dreams and plans were taken seriously. There seemed to be a tacit understanding among people that helping others to gain more power over their lives would in turn help them along their own path, suggesting mutuality in that the others' well-being was constitutive of their own. There was reciprocity in that people with disabilities had opportunities to do things for others. It was apparent too that labelled people in these kinds of situations spoke in a different voice when talking about their homes, their dreams, and their work—the voice heard when people who are not labelled speak, people who feel they have a place in the world, and who feel they have a future. As we listened to the ways service providers talked to and about the people they served, we learned what sorts of social relationships they had with those people; and it was clear which relationships were characterized by caring and unconditional acceptance.

The experiences of those who participated in the study strongly support the conclusions, first, that empowerment is a natural result of people's lives having *texture;* and second, that texture arises when the individual finds a secure place and a rich life in the community and is fully accepted there—so that, to reiterate the construct first introduced in chapter 1, he or she enjoys *empowerment-in-community*. By texture, then, we mean that people have social and physical variety and richness in their day-to-day experiences. Their days are varied, and although they may have an activity that they routinely engage in at least for part of any day, there is also a sense of choice in what they are involved in from week to week. There is more spontaneity in day-to-day life, and routine activities bring the individual into contact with a wide variety of people and lead to a wide variety of experiences. Leisure pursuits, for instance, include friends, family, and staff at various times, and in different venues. People whose lives have texture may indeed have part of their day organized around their disability and the special needs it creates, but this does not define the whole of their existence. For a person's life to have notable texture, it is important that he or she interact as well with people from the community and that these interactions be founded on mutual caring and respect and involve a measure of permanence. This is to say that the conditions that bring texture into the lives of people with disabilities are the same as those that bring texture into the lives of people generally.

By contrast, people whose lives lack texture spend almost their entire time in a world that is defined by disability and that is tightly programmed, with little or no individual choice and differentiation. Their basic needs, such as shelter, food, clothing, and something to do in their work and leisure time, may very well be met. But there is little variation or diversity, and their day-to-day experiences are structured by the human service system. To the extent that this is the case, the promise held out by the deinstitutionalization movement has not been realized. Moving from a total institution into the community may represent a significant advance, but a life in the community that is wholly defined by disability lacks texture, just as did life within the walls of the institution. As people have moved out of institutional settings, what has often been difficult to avoid is a constriction of the individual's points of access into the wider community, with the result that, for people with disabilities, the community is experienced as an "institution without walls."

An understanding of power as sharing, respect, and reciprocity in support relationships is intricately linked with the idea of a textured life. We want now to look more closely at this linkage. Why does the sort of empowerment that a textured life brings depend on a person maintaining with others symbiotic relations of sharing and mutual support? More generally, since a textured life primarily requires transcending the world of disability to become a participating member of the wider community, what explains the relevance of social integration and mutual growth and development to empowerment? To answer these questions, we turn now to a consideration of the conditions for a textured life, as these may be inferred from our conversations with individuals who are developmentally disabled.

Mutuality and the Conditions for a Textured Life

As we have said, the social ecological theory of empowerment is associated with two key contentions. First, empowerment does not depend on domination, by which one person gains exclusive control over resources. Instead, it is by entering into symbiotic relations with one another, relations of sharing and *mutuality*, that people become empowered. Second, an empowered person's life is characterized by *texture*. By understanding the conditions on which texture in a life depends, we are able to understand as well the linkage between these two key contentions, and thereby the inevitability of the central thesis of this study, empowerment-in-community. In this chapter, we shall identify some conditions for a person's life having texture. Each brings that individual into the community in a distinctive way.

A textured life exists in the presence of what we have been able to identify as four fairly specific conditions: *knowledge, aspirations, social commitment,* and *openness*. Where people's lives reflected some but perhaps not all of these conditions, their lives had less texture and the level to which empowerment was evident was similarly tempered.

Knowledge

The role of knowledge in leading to power has long been recognized. Equally important is the ability to act upon the knowledge one has. Knowledge of how human service systems and policies are devised and operationalized is a significant factor in the kind of support a person ultimately receives. Policies are often complex and difficult to negotiate. For adults with developmental disabilities, gaining access to this knowledge may present additional challenges. Some individuals benefit considerably from having support persons connected to them who have an in-depth knowledge and understanding of the system and a clear commitment to support the individual in the utilization of that knowledge. This was clear among the adults with developmental disabilities and their families who participated in this study. Family members worked hard to secure knowledge and then to apply this knowledge in ways that could respond to the needs of their sons or daughters.

One woman had been actively involved for many years in planning and advocacy in her "home" province, where she used the services of a traditional transfer agency in supporting her son:

Clara, Richard's mother
For seventeen years he was in a segregated school and for the last three years we integrated him into a local high school. It was difficult to find a right kind of program so I was sitting on a board, I was sitting on a committee that put this program in place and we had to be where the action is so we finally accessed it.
(Microboard)

After hearing "via the grapevine" of the availability of individualized funding in another province, she decided to make that move. By the time we met her she had been able to secure individualized funding and set up a microboard for her son. Without the in-depth understanding of "the system" that she gained through her earlier experiences and efforts to gain services for her son, she likely would not have had the knowledge that enabled her to do this.

Another parent who had once worked for a large agency in her community, had developed a private, for-profit agency. This agency differed in significant ways from traditional public agencies and from the microboard approach to support in that it was run along the lines of a private enterprise with individuals and their families essentially purchasing services. The owner of the agency explained that her son's needs lay behind her determination and drive in developing this service, which she was more able to do because of the knowledge she had acquired earlier through working in the system:

Claudette
We are a business. The reason we are a business was a philosophical decision on my part. Because Sam [her son] had always been served through the goodness and charity of agencies where you are fundraising all the time, I wanted him to have the dignity of purchasing services from a legitimate, not that charities aren't legitimate, but it was just a different focus. I wanted also for our service to be one that could apply to any type of population. It wasn't specific to individuals with a disability with mental handicaps. Not that profit is our motive by any stretch of the imagination, it was more to get away from the idea that it is being a charity.
(Owner; private, for-profit agency)

It was evident that knowledge was relevant not just to the individuals and families, but also to others in that social context, such as paid support and informal support people. In addition, associated with the microboards that participated in

this study were ministry personnel. Though not actually members of the microboard, ministry personnel acted within that social context in ways that proved
helpful and liberating to the members. One family explained how, after connecting
with the ministry and gaining access to knowledge and resources, things changed
dramatically in their lives:

> Melanie, Josephine's mother
> *[F]or two years we fought and then set up the microboard. But I must say, the
> Ministry was very generous and they have been absolutely great. I mean, like you
> met Kent [Ministry staff], and they are way more aware of what is needed and they
> really get to know the person they serve and know that person's needs.*
> (Daughter supported by microboard)

The power of knowledge, and the ability to use it in fulfilling a commitment toward improving the life situation of the individual, were most apparent in
the case of the microboard approach to support. The value of being connected to
a network of support such as family members, paid support, and informal social
support from the community was emphasized by one woman who was part of a
microboard:

> Mary, member of Kate's microboard
> *Well see, that is the power of having the connections with the network too. You
> know you get to hear about stuff that you might not see in the newspaper or hear
> about otherwise. It's really valuable.*
> (Microboard)

Those who had been able to gain access to knowledge and had been able
to put that knowledge to work—that is, to act on the knowledge and use it in ways
that produced helpful results—had a strong sense of a "future," both for themselves
and for those they supported. In contrast, where support staff had relatively
minimal understanding and knowledge of the system, they tended to lack
optimism. When asked what sort of future she envisaged for the people she
supported, a woman who supervised a community-based day program responded:

> Lynn, day program manager
> *Progress and go from here? I would like to say, "Yes," but I don't know where
> they can go from here. I don't know what their options are. I don't know what the
> resources are for them, that is where I have the problem in saying, "Okay, you
> have done your job here; you need to move on," because I don't know where they
> move on to. So I keep them forever.*
> (Private, for-profit agency)

This support worker saw no future for people beyond the segregated day program she managed; neither had she considered other opportunities that existed in the community. In contrast, other study participants, most especially those associated with the microboard approach to support, had knowledge and understanding of "how things worked." These people seemed better prepared to search out yet more information on other opportunities and resources that added texture to people's lives. It was essentially a cumulative process and it was as though people's sense of potency and energy grew stronger with each success they and those around them experienced.

Aspirations

People whose lives had texture were more ready to have "dreams" for their future, more able to imagine a life in which they could and would have significant work opportunities, meaningful relationships, and a feeling of something they could aim for in living a full life. In addition, those around the person had an awareness of what might be possible in people's lives. We think of this in terms of aspirations: the ability and willingness to visualize a bright future, along with a desire to grow and to experience those possibilities.

A long history of struggles to overcome barriers to full participation in the life of our communities has doubtless influenced people's confidence about their ability to achieve and grow in mainstream society. But many people we talked with were determined to overcome the obstacles and find the best possible alternative. This was especially so for family members who had held onto their dreams for their sons and daughters. A mother whose daughter faced considerable challenges said:

> Janet, Sarah's mother
> *My dreams for her are no different than my dreams for my son and my grandchildren: that she feel fulfilled; that she has a sense of belonging and accomplishment. Whatever it is, that she feels that she has been a contributor. I think for life I would like her to be living in a place where she is respected and accepted and valued; that she has choice; that she has the opportunity not to be so impoverished that she can't travel, that she can't do some things. I want her to have a rich life. I don't want to be the caregiver, the primary caregiver. I didn't want to live with my mother much beyond the time I was fifteen or sixteen. I can't imagine it would be any different for her.*
> (Public, non-profit agency)

This was particularly problematic when those who were paid to provide support did not see the person's strengths and potential, and so unwittingly operated in ways which strengthened rather than broke down those barriers. As a result, all too often the individuals who perhaps would have most benefited from the support were unable to summon a motivating vision of a "bright future." While the mother in this case had high hopes for her daughter, those aspirations were not shared by the worker, and absence of mutuality was evident.

Against considerable odds, and despite lack of encouragement from support workers who thought it important to be "realistic," some individuals managed to hold on to their dreams. A support worker who was asked whether the man he supported might not one day acquire a driver's licence responded:

Bill, support worker to Ron
No, and he would love to. He thinks he's going to get one. When you sit down and be realistic with him, he'll accept it for a while, but then after a while again he'll get the urge to say, "Oh no, I'm going to go for my driver's licence." Or, "I want to be an air pilot." Or, "I want to be a DJ." There are certain requirements you need to be able to do those kind of things. I think the biggest thing is responsibility, and what their mental capacity is able to handle. That's where I think sometimes I think they get stuck. But if there is one thing they want, it's to be like you or I, in the sense of having a full-time job, a house, a truck, get married, have children, things like that. That's the biggest thing they miss. Even though they are mentally challenged people and are slower in certain aspects, they are smart enough to know they would like those things.
(Private, for-profit agency)

In contrast to those who stopped simply at empathy, staff who shared people's belief in their ability and who were committed to helping them improve their quality of life greatly facilitated their attempt to realize their dreams.

Sandy, support worker to Keith
He has been dreaming to go and visit his sister [in Australia]. He has been trying to save all his money. It was his decision not to go to camp. Karen [a worker] has really been advocating for Keith to raise funds other than what he gets on his FBA money. So he has had people involved to give donations. There was a newspaper article to ask for donations to help him. So he is really hoping. . . . We will do everything we can to make that goal for him. One staff person moved to Australia and she came back to visit. So Keith was excited because now he can see his sister and her when he goes.
(Public, non-profit agency)

People who are disabled have traditionally faced considerable socio-economic disadvantages, and so for this man to even contemplate raising the funds to travel to Australia would have been virtually impossible without those around him believing in his dream and advocating for him. His case was like that of many study participants who spent their working days in sheltered workshops, otherwise designated as training centres, where they were paid token amounts which had no relation to legislated minimum wage rates. The inequity of it all did not go unnoticed, although few felt able to voice their concern. When they did, one had the sense that the inequity had to be accepted as a fact of life.

> Judy
> *I can't live on it. If I had to live on the money I get paid here [from workshop], I couldn't live on it, but it's something to do. After you have your bills and groceries, I don't have much left. And I like to go out, I'm not one to stay in my apartment. . . . There's a lot of things to pay before the end of the month and I don't have enough money most of the time.*
> (Supported by public, non-profit agency)

This individual's situation was typical of that of those who were essentially supported by the transfer agency with program funding. She received her family benefits allowance cheque each month, which covered the bare essentials of life, and then the workshop paid her a token amount each week. As she said, it gave her "something to do." There was little else in her life to aspire to and she couldn't imagine life without the workshop.

A significant factor in people's lives was whether their aspirations were shared by others in their circle of support. On occasion, some of these people could not, or at least did not, convey the same hopeful sense of a future that existed elsewhere in the circle, as in the case of the mother and support worker who spoke of their very different aspirations. But when social support emanating from family members, paid support, and others manifested itself in mutually reinforcing ways, there was respect for the person's interests and abilities. Those in the social context saw the person as having abilities and aspirations which were no different from their own or from those of non-disabled citizens.

> Mary, member of Kate's microboard
> *I'm here as part of the microboard, so I am formally not a caregiver as such. I no longer am paid to be in Kate's life. I am here as a volunteer because we are friends and because I think it's just great. You know she's going to get to move on, on her own. And [part of why I'm here is] because I have a vision of what I want to see for my own son, too.*
> (Microboard)

Sharing in aspirations for a bright future was most often found in those members of the circle of support who were deeply imbued with social commitment, including commitment to the person with a disability at the centre of the circle.

Social Commitment

The nature of the relationship people have with those who provide support to them is central to their sense of well-being. In the absence of commitment, the relationship will be less satisfactory for the individual and for those in the support role. Social commitment exists where the support for the person who has a disability is based on unconditional acceptance, endures challenge, and is sustainable.

Closely related to the notion of unconditional acceptance is whether the people working together actually like each other. Generally, when there is talk about the desirability of "unconditional acceptance" of people within human services, stress is not placed on the importance of *liking* the person. Among the service providers who participated in this study, there appeared to be an unspoken understanding—either that the support worker and the person being supported liked one another, as though it were a given; or alternatively, that it was really irrelevant whether or not they liked one another. A few support workers seemed to consciously recognize this aspect of providing support, although it was rarely acknowledged by senior administrators that disliking a person can lead to significant difficulties for both the support person and the individual being supported.

James, support worker to George and Elizabeth
Well, there's a few clients I don't necessarily like. I don't think you have to like someone, necessarily, to work with them. I don't think it's possible, because they need help that almost goes hand in hand with them not being likeable to a degree. I mean, likeable means that you've got your life under control, and you're good looking, and you speak well, and you have a good sense of humour. I mean, most of those are not going to exist beforehand in a lot of people. I don't worry about liking. I think it's more a question of, "Can I work with them?" And that means are they going to push so many buttons of mine that I can just remain detached from that or am I going to not be able to remain detached? So far, I have been able to just remain detached. It's not easy, I mean, I do have a hard time with bodily stuff. Like one guy drooling down the front of his mouth all over his shirt, I'll admit that's one of the really hard things for me. I don't handle that well, or maybe I do but it's harder, I have to work harder.
(Private, for-profit agency)

Some staff had come to like an individual, but were prepared to admit that it had not been an easy process. A worker commented on her feelings about a woman with severe disabilities that she supported:

Judy, Bev's live-in caregiver
She needs a one-on-one. And we have tried alternative programming and it just didn't work. And so Bev's been in [the agency] and it's worked so far the best. Now, unfortunately, we have gone through quite a few day people due to the fact that burnout, and Bev is and can be a handful. And you really have to like Bev to work with her. And a lot of times that doesn't just come naturally; like I mean, I'll even tell you that it took me a while to like Bev. When I first got her and I was

dealing with a lot of very hard realities. If I did not have Jill [Bev's mother] to support me, and I'm being honest, if I did not have Jill, she would have been gone. In the sense of, "Jill, she's doing this, does that mean I'm no good, is that ok?" And Jill will say, "Oh no, she does that all the time." So then I started feeling more comfortable with her, so it just depends.
(Support worker; private, for-profit agency)

     The nature of the support relationship was quite distinct when people who were paid to provide support not only exhibited unconditional acceptance of the individual, but as well showed unmistakably that they liked and respected the person. Of course it might be said that to the extent liking and respect are absent, acceptance is not possible. Equally important was presence of mutuality and respect, reflected in the way support staff talked about and interacted with the people they supported. When questioned about the non-hierarchical dynamic that was evident between herself and an individual she supported, one staff person said:

Sandy, support worker to Keith
I try very hard, and no matter who I support I think that they are all capable, and can do anything as long as they have adequate support, any type of support. We may not be able to give the one-to-one 40 hours a week; [if we could] they would be able to flourish. I think it depends on how comfortable the staff person is, and they [person supported] have to know it's okay, that I'm not perfect. I think it is his personality. There are some people that I support that do need more structure, not all the time, but they do need more support. I think it is very individualized.
(Public, non-profit agency)

     Not every agency provides for such sensitivity to individual differences, particularly when they are funded to provide programs serving large numbers of people. As well, not every support worker is able to practise with such reflection. Where support was individualized, as in the case of microboards, it was generally more realistic for families and individuals to seek out support staff whose strengths and capabilities more closely matched the support requirements. The growth and rewards that emanated from the relationship were reciprocated and mutually reinforcing among people within the individual's social environment. Jean's attitude illustrates the point:

Jean, support person/companion to Josephine
I would only see myself as Josephine's helper, just helping her out in her daily needs that she needs help with. I don't see myself as a daily worker with Jo. I've been friends with Jo for six years and I'm in and out every day, whether I'm off or on. . . . I find it hard when people even ask, "What is your job?" you know; it is just, I don't see it that way at all.
(Microboard)

Social commitment characterized relationships some people had with those who provided both formal and informal support, and it existed in a range of support relationships, including those with friends and paid staff. Most evident, however, in relationships where continuity and ongoing commitment were present, such as in the case above, was that the structure of the support service allowed for individual choice and a richness in everyday life experiences. The microboard approach enabled people who shared a genuine friendship and mutual liking to be paid for the formal support they provided to the individual. This does not mean that other mechanisms, such as in the traditional transfer agency, deny the possibility of support workers liking the people they are paid to support. In the latter instance though, there are systemic impediments to continuity and a sharing of commitment among people. These impediments may exist when, as is usually the case, paid support persons in traditional human service settings are required to demonstrate accountability to the employer, who generally is not the person with a disability. As well, in these instances, the support is seen more as a part of one's employment, part of the job, in contrast to a commitment to an individual.

Openness

While these conditions—knowledge, aspirations, and social commitment—were identified in a number of different human service settings, they contributed more to the individual's empowerment when they existed in tandem with an approach to service which involved openness to the community as a whole. Richness and texture were dependent on the individual having access to, and opportunities to participate in, the life of the community; that is, on the community being open to him or her. In one sense, then, openness was the most important of the four conditions discussed here and the other three mainly served to make openness possible or to enable the individual to take advantage of it. The knowledge that really counts is knowledge concerning these opportunities. The aspirations that really count are aspirations to take on the challenges such opportunities present. The social commitment that really counts envisages the person to whom one is committed finding a rich and textured life in the community, a life that gives substance to the ideal of empowerment-in-community.

Unfortunately, however, many people, regardless of the type of agency that supported them, were living in the community, but were not really part of the community. Staff whose sense of community did not encompass anything beyond the service system did little to facilitate and encourage involvement with people beyond the world of disability. For the vast majority, life revolved around service systems and supports that were directed only at people with disabilities.

In many cases, although there was some evidence of texture in the person's life, this was limited because his or her life experiences remained within a world of disability. Attempts to reach beyond the microcosm of the human service agency in terms of meaningful involvements with the community as a whole did not occur unless those around the person were ready to seek out opportunities that provided texture to the person's life. Staff had recognized the significance of this for Paul, and his interest became their interest as they linked to the community and in turn brought texture to his life:

> Martha, support worker to Paul
> *Paul has perfect rhythm. No, he's not good at learning the actual steps but he has perfect rhythm and he is a perfect gentleman. And he is very well liked at that noon-hour country line dancing. And he went to another country line dancing class for disabled and didn't like it. . . . So that was toasted. That didn't happen. But we went to the Corral three weeks ago and did country line dancing. It was hilarious. It was fun.*
> (Private, for-profit agency)

The ability to venture beyond the context of support services by opening the community to the individual and the individual to the community became critical in understanding why some individuals had richness and texture in their lives. Microboards had the greatest success in this regard, particularly when openness was conjoined with the other conditions that collectively made for empowerment. The microboards were based on social commitment—that is, they offered the person with a disability unconditional acceptance and support and tended to ensure that this same unconditional acceptance would be forthcoming from his or her support persons, whether paid or unpaid. As well, members of the microboard shared hopes and dreams for the person's future, and provided knowledge and an open path to the broader community beyond the world of disability. It was this path or link which offered the foundation for a textured life.

> Jean, support person/companion to Josephine
> *Yeah, Jo's friend Terry, and a friend Karl, we usually call them to go to the bars. They are the guy friends that are our little bodyguards when Josephine and I are too scared to go to the karaoke at night and to help play pool, and to teach Josephine and I to play pool and stuff. They go out with us into the bars and the beaches and everything. Call them and they come and visit Josephine and bring her Valentine stuff. . . . In the summer, Josephine has a flower garden that she helps us with and she takes flowers to all her friends and brings them up to the hospital to people that she has known over the years. She takes them to the people at the elderly homes and stuff like that. Yeah, Jo is very active, she knows a lot of people in town, a lot of people know Josephine. She admires them, they admire her. She's very busy.*
> (Microboard)

The fact that the microboard is relatively small, usually four to six people, helps the group to maintain its energy and focus on the individual with a disability.

This focussing on the individual with a disability also accounts for the symbiotic relationship that emerges among the members— the individual is at the centre of the collective, and when that person begins to flourish and prosper, so, too, do the other members of the microboard.

This supports the view expressed earlier, that empowerment is not a zero-sum game in which for every winner there must be a loser. Instead, as one becomes empowered others who are part of the same social context with that person experience empowerment as well. The evidence is fairly compelling from the experiences of people who participated in this study—when individuals with disabilities become more empowered, those around them appear to be more full of hope and energy than is the case for those who support individuals who seem not to be making similar progress. The sometimes very poignant comments people made to us about their work and their commitment to those they supported pointed to this generalization: to the degree the four conditions are absent from the social context which surrounds the individual with a disability, not just that person, but also the others in that context, fail to flourish.

Chapter 7

TOWARD A NEW PERSPECTIVE
ON SOCIAL SUPPORT

In this closing chapter, we shall describe an alternative way of structuring policy and practice which we think will bring us closer to achieving empowerment-in-community for adults with developmental disabilities. Our intention is not so much to recommend specific policy changes as to identify a new perspective on social support capable of informing a change in policy direction. This perspective is suggested by what we have learned from our conversations with adults with developmental disabilities, their families, friends, and support people—what we have learned about both the weaknesses and the strengths of the current support system. We begin with a brief account of the ways that system is failing those it is intended to support, focussing on governmental failures and the failures of the dominant model of support.

This discussion is informed by the account, provided in the preceding chapter, of the four conditions for bringing texture to people's lives—knowledge, aspirations, social commitment, and openness. As we shall see, the dominant model of support fails because it is not well adapted to securing those conditions. What recommends the new perspective on support is that it is specifically grounded in those conditions.

Failures of Government

In the last decade of this millennium, Canadian human services of all kinds are undergoing massive restructuring. Many definitions and assumptions once taken as givens have been rethought. Many have attacked the presumption that people with developmental disabilities are deficient, unable to contribute to society, pitiable, and best hidden away. Concurrently, over the last twenty years, we have heard criticism of systems based on "maintenance," where it is assumed people with developmental disabilities are incapable of moving forward, and so the emphasis is on providing quality service to maintain them. Parallel with this we have heard criticism of the "readiness model," which assumes that people have to be made ready before they can venture forward from the world of disability and segregated programming into the mainstream world beyond. Some progress toward ensuring people with disabilities were able to live more as other members of society live occurred as policy makers and service providers sought frameworks that granted labelled individuals the status of citizens, and focussed on securing their rights and building their capacities. This has been reflected in legal decisions (Rioux, Bach, & Crawford, 1997), in human rights legislation, and in the missions and mandates of human service agencies.

The results of our study, however, suggest that large-scale implementation of supports that focus on rights and capacities of labelled people have lagged behind the rhetoric. "Quality service" and the "readiness" models that Luckasson and Spitalnik (1994) talked about do in fact still hold sway over the majority of Canadian services for people with developmental disabilities. In part, the slow spread of the community living vision is due to another significant historical trend. Over the last fifteen years, governments have scaled back their role in providing support to marginalized people generally. In the era of institutions, and even for several years after deinstitutionalization began, many believed support for people with developmental disabilities was secure in the social welfare system, which was presumed to be entrenched in this country. However, preoccupation with deficit reduction has led to a reduction and restructuring of public services. Some support services have reemerged from the restructuring as privatized industries. The preoccupation with deficit reduction and the emergence of privatization in human services have meant that making a profit from provision of support is becoming part of a revised definition of social support. These factors have led to greater uncertainty for individuals and families than ever before: service providers begin to think differently when there is a profit to be made from their services, and thus they may serve only those "clients" from whom there is greater assurance that they will actually realize a profit. The entrenchment of the client status, an issue to which we shall return shortly, presents additional ambiguities for individuals and families who at one point in our history would have been relatively assured of societal commitment to their well-being through a strong system of social welfare.

Failure of the Dominant Model of Support

The movement toward for-profit provision of support has not seriously threatened the dominance of the traditional model of support, however. Under this model, programs which institutions once offered to adults with developmental disabilities are now located in the community in the guise of a community-based system of supports. But from the perspective of the individual who is supported, there are two important similarities to the earlier institutional model. First, by and large these programs are specifically "programs for the disabled," so that participation in them does not offer a pathway into the larger community. They establish within the larger community a subworld of disability. As a result, the dominant model creates a closed system and does not support the openness that we identified in the preceding chapter as the critical condition for securing texture in people's lives. Second, the programs are fixed, and typically they are not malleable to the individual's needs or preferences. At best, they are there *for* him or her. More often, however, they are a Procrustean bed of standardized programs to which the individual must adapt.

In the preceding chapters we have reviewed the sometimes chaotic ways in which this new community-based system of supports has evolved. Dramatic and often poorly understood shifts in values and philosophies about how support should work, coupled with the erosion of government support for social welfare, has left the original vision of the community living movement susceptible to dilution, misinterpretation, and even conscious co-optation. But even when these problems are not felt, the community-based system of supports remains an essentially closed system and one that is paternalistically offered up to the supported individuals. This means that it contributes little to the texture of people's lives. It does not lead to empowerment-in-community.

It should not be surprising that in a closed and paternalistic service system, workers often take "ownership" of the individuals they support. This notion of staff taking ownership of the individual is not new (see, for example, Roeher Institute, 1990). Often, staff essentially took control of individuals and exercised enormous power over most aspects of their lives. It was evident in the way staff related with them that some were treated as commodities by the system. All of this increases people's vulnerability. Particularly disturbing were those instances where parents seemed so desperate to know their son or daughter would be cared for when they die that they would tolerate what we identified to be inappropriate approaches to support from workers. Parents often were cautious, not wanting to "make a fuss," for fear of losing what little support they did have. Hence, considerable numbers of people with disabilities, along with their families, were dependent upon others for a determination of what they could or could not aspire to and what sort of future they might face.

The result was that within the traditional service system, most people had limited options. They worked in sheltered or volunteer situations. They lived and socialized primarily with their peers who also had disabilities. Some spent much of their leisure time with paid people. Their world was predominantly encircled with others who either received support or provided support. That said, for many, the involvements they had with their peers was very important to their general sense of well-being. They enjoyed this aspect of their lives, it provided stability and continuity, and these people formed the hub of community. It was equally the case, however, that people very often appeared powerless to become active and involved with the rest of the community and with others beyond the service system. Unfortunately, all too often, attitudes of support staff exacerbated this sense of powerlessness. Staff often had no vision of what was possible for those to whom they provided support and were content to see these individuals continue to be confined to the world of disability. In terms of the previous account of conditions for texture in people's lives, openness, knowledge, aspiration, and social commitment were lacking.

It has long been understood that lack of access to valued resources is a critical aspect of powerlessness, and that empowerment involves working towards more equitable distributions (Parenti, 1978). The introduction of alternative funding mechanisms, such as indirect individualized funding, occurred in large measure as a response to recognizing people's powerlessness within the traditional service system. Here funds are placed with an agency, but earmarked to provide services specifically in response to the requirements of each person supported by the agency. However, as we observed, in areas where people received indirect individualized funding, their decision-making power was severely constrained by the fact that decisions about their lives remained with others. All of the people we met who were supported by indirect individualized funding received their services from for-profit agencies. Some had public trustees who had ultimate veto power over the disposal of their income, which was used in the purchase of services from these agencies. Many of these individuals led relatively uniform lives. Like those within the traditional service system, they worked in sheltered workshops or volunteer enclaves, they socialized and recreated with others who were similarly supported, and they spent much of their spare time with people who were paid to support them. They may have lived in smaller residential settings, often with a live-in caregiver, but it was not at all clear that their lives were any more individualized or that they were more empowered than their counterparts who were supported in non-profit agencies and lived in group homes with three or four other people. We are convinced that before the potential of more equitable distributions of resources can be realized, there needs to be a shift in the way social support functions, so that reciprocity and mutuality are possible.

Relationships That Anchor Us in Community

While we are critical of a traditional service system that maintains people in programs, and that generally does not provide pathways to the community that take the individual beyond the service system, it must be said that in its implementation the system is not all bad. Specifically, in some segregated living and working situations, people related with each other in ways that demonstrated the value they placed on their relationships and on the mutual support that existed within the group. For instance, at one agency we visited, the line between some staff and some supported persons was blurred as role definition became hazy and the differentiation between paid support person and support recipient began to break down. The relationship between staff and the individual moved beyond the worker/client understanding as determined by traditional role definitions. The agency leadership here had been quite deliberate in its adoption of "self-directed" teams throughout the agency. Under this approach, some individuals who attended the agency's workshop, who would otherwise be regarded as "clients," at least temporarily stepped out of that role and were able to contribute more as a support person to others in that setting. The caring that existed amongst members in the workshop was striking, as was the importance people placed on contributing to the well-being of others. The *sense* of community in that environment went hand in hand with social commitment between people. Despite this, constraints inherent in the traditional service system appeared to block people here from achieving textured lives. We'll return to this consideration shortly in thinking about "when people flourish."

Reviews of approaches to building friendships for people with disabilities (Roeher Institute, 1990) affirm that true friendships tend to occur when people feel valued and appreciated for who they are as people, when they feel they are "givers" as well as "receivers," and when they share information and feelings openly. Friendships are seen as critical resources for people with disabilities, in part because they represent windows of opportunity for expanding one's social circle beyond the confines of the disability services system, offering vitality and texture to people's lives.

To understand this, one must have in mind that although the traditional service system structures the environment of individuals who have a disability so that, as we say, they live "within a world of disability," the individuals within that world are not totally defined by their disability. Rather, the disability is but one feature of their complete selves. (And, if truth be told, in a wider sense, everyone is marked by a disability of some sort, even though not all are labelled.) Because of this, when two people who have been labelled achieve a rounded friendship, the world they enter through that friendship transcends the world of disability somewhat. This occurs because in their friendship they make connection with traits of one another by which they transcend their disability.

Relationships between persons with disabilities were respected and valued in several of the sites visited. These included reciprocity and caring for fellow members. In some social contexts, people developed caring relationships which provided stability and feelings of belonging. As well, where authentic friendships emerged between an individual and a person who was paid to provide support to him or her, we witnessed a richness and quality of life which were undeniably good. In the past, researchers and visionaries working in the field of disability have suggested that both of these forms of human connection—that is, more than casual relationships between disabled peers, and friendships between staff and supported individuals—are troublesome and inappropriate. It has been further suggested that power differentials can never be removed from within the human service structure. However, the stories that people told, the accounts of their lives and of what mattered to them, were undeniably convincing in terms of the real value of these relationships. This led us to the conviction that it would be wrong to discourage authentic relationships among people with disabilities and those who support them.

It is obvious, however, that authentic relationships which reflect social commitment have, on their own, only limited potential in sustaining a textured life. Such relationships may do nothing more than make an otherwise intolerable situation barely tolerable. Regardless of how satisfying their relationships may be, the fact that individuals supported within traditional agency structures are dependent upon predetermined programs for support, limits their aspirations and their ability to act on knowledge that might connect them with the world beyond services for people with disabilities. What appears necessary, then, is a new approach that breaks down dependence and provides pathways to the wider community.

Since our account of this new approach will involve extensive reference to microboards, it might be helpful to preface the account with a reminder concerning the basic features of microboards and how microboards differ from the traditional boards of public transfer agencies. The microboard model of support has some elements in common with these traditional boards, yet it is decidedly different. A significant difference is that traditional boards are usually quite large and their members very often have little or no contact with the people being supported by the agencies. The microboard generally comprises four to six members who have a strong association and involvement with the person with a disability. The person receives direct individualized funding, whereby dollars are allocated according to the amount of support he or she needs in order to be a full participant in community life. The microboard members—who may be members of the person's family, including parents, brothers and sisters, and advocates and friends, possibly professionals such as teachers, or simply other interested individuals from the community in which the person lives—assist in managing the resources, financial and otherwise, that are available to the individual. They work collectively with the individual to develop a support plan and go out into the community to link with the support and services identified as helpful to the person. The members are responsible for the management of the microboard, including funding. Most importantly, though, they are accountable to the person being supported.

Microboards and a New Model of Support

Openness can be understood in two complementary ways. First, we may think of the community as presenting to the individual a number of doors, entrances to the varied life of the community. Insofar as these doors are capable of being opened, the community is open: the individual is able to participate in the life of the community and thus may have a sense of belonging. As suggested in chapter 1, in the discussion of personal and social dimensions of empowerment, whether these doors are capable of being opened is only partly a matter of having a legal right to enter. Equally, it is a matter of possessing the means and ability to engage in the life behind the doors and of being encouraged to enter and of being welcomed in. This forms, as it were, the outsider-looking-in perspective.

But from a complementary perspective, openness refers to the structure or "world" one inhabits within the community. This forms, as it were, the insider-looking-out perspective. The question now is whether that structure is porous. Are there pathways that lead from it into the larger community? Or does it enclose one in a possibly paternalistic embrace? For example, one of the aspects of the so-called "culture of poverty" is that it places one in a world that closes itself on the wider community that surrounds it. It blocks off the pathways to that wider community, despite the fact that the wider community may be in many important respects very open, as seen from the first perspective. Nevertheless, the wider community is not really open, because it does nothing or little to break down the culture of poverty, and so open pathways to the wider community.

The dominant model of support for adults with developmental disabilities puts in place a service system that is closed in this second sense. Like the culture of poverty, it creates an enclosed world that offers few pathways out into the wider community. No doubt there is a great deal that the wider community could do to welcome and encourage participation by adults with developmental disabilities, so that it might become more fully open in the first-mentioned sense. But until the dominant model of support that creates this enclosed world is replaced by a model that envisages and encourages open pathways out into the wider community, openness will not be achieved, and the lives of adults with developmental disabilities will lack texture.

What recommends the microboard model of support in this connection is that it is essentially an open structure. The person with a disability is at the centre of the microboard. Microboard members are there specifically to enable the individual with the disability to engage with the wider community. They are, as it were, conduits whose role it is to break down, overcome, or get around the barriers that would otherwise enclose the individual within a world of disability. Knowledge is the principal vehicle and social commitment and aspirations supply the energy and motivation. Since the person is publically funded on an individual basis through a grant the microboard receives, the model avoids the actual or threatening paternalism of the dominant model. Hence, whereas in the dominant model, traditional programs and the system are at the centre, in the microboard model, social support is directed to the *person* at the centre.

When People Flourish

Shared knowledge, aspirations, social commitment, and openness bring to microboards, at their best, that richness of experience which we identify as a textured life. For instance, a most distinctive aspect of the microboard approach to social support in contrast to the more traditional approaches to service provision, was the way those in the individual's social context responded to change and growth in the life of the person they were supporting. Because of the interactive nature of the four conditions of a textured life, and the role each member played in realizing those conditions, those supporting the individual appeared to experience a collective enhancement of well-being. We have called this a *social ecological* theory of empowerment—as the individual flourishes, so does the collective which forms a significant part of that individual's social environment.

There is some similarity between these ideas and those that Carniol (1995) was speaking about in his work on "social empathy." In describing the need for social workers to become "case critical," i.e., critical of conventional social work and related therapies, he suggests that workers make linkages, as well as assist the people they work with to make linkages, between their experiences and challenges and those faced by others in similar personal and political circumstances. Hence, rather than individualistic remedies, solutions are sought which respond to collective needs and interests. Carniol believes this leads to the empowerment of the counsellor and the client: as the counsellor sees the client gaining strength and growing in motivation, self-confidence and self-esteem, the counsellor experiences growth and positive change in his or her personal situation. In effect, then, the counsellor ceases to perceive the individual as a "client" in the traditional sense. In order for this to begin to happen in the case of the individuals we met with, the worker/client distinction has to be redefined and the social context reconstructed to allow for the emergence of social commitment. In the case of the one traditional agency where management had encouraged this, social commitment was evident in some relationships, but in the absence of the other conditions—knowledge, aspirations, and openness—the texture of people's lives remained limited, and they were unable to move definitively beyond the worker/client role differentiation.

For marginalized individuals, the status of clienthood has been identified as maintaining the power differential that keeps them in the dependent role (Saul, 1995). A typical outcome of perceiving oneself as a "client" is that feelings of inadequacy become permanent, so that positive change and growth become unattainable. It was only among microboards that there was a noticeable absence of the status of "clienthood." "Clienthood" implies a power differential. But individualized funding in combination with the power of the collective tended to put the microboard and the person with a disability at its centre on an equal footing with those with whom they interacted. Each member had a critical role to play in the overall well-being of the microboard; between them there was insight and understanding of the social and political context in which the individual and the microboard existed. That knowledge was itself empowering; being able to directly access the resources, human and otherwise, to *act* on the knowledge, furthered members' sense of accomplishment and engagement. This, in turn, allowed for the sharing of aspirations and a strong sense of a promising future, with each member having the ability to offer a connection or pathway to the community-at-large. Each member drew strength from his or her ability to contribute to the successes experienced by the collective, which in turn sustained the social context. This is in stark contrast to the impotence experienced by many individuals and family members who essentially remain as "outsiders" to the system of programs that exist to serve clients with disabilities and for whom community remains unconnected and remote.

Accountability and the Public Good

As Racino (1994) noted, "new concepts need to develop from an understanding more strongly based on such principles as self-determination, mutual decision-making and social justice" (p.188). From the perspective of a social ecological theory of empowerment, it is imperative that mutual decision-making extend into the realm of economic deliberations; in particular, stakeholders must be included in decisions around funding. In his theory of public action, Handler (1986) focussed attention on the interrelationship of policy development and implementation—public action means that policy formulation and implementation are parts of one process. The social autonomy of participants in discretionary decisions depends on their continuous involvement in that ongoing process rather than in isolated and disjointed pursuits.

While in some jurisdictions there appear to be efforts to develop a more participatory process in the provision of services to persons with developmental disabilities, participation in policy and planning decisions continues to be selective in terms of social movement group representation. This representation should not stop at the critical point where policy formulation and implementation come together; that is, in decisions regarding commitment of funds. The approach adopted in the development of the microboards that were part of this study allows for active participation in policy formulation and implementation, including commitment of funds. Microboard members representing the interests of the person with a disability, along with the bureaucracy representing the public interest, were present at the point where policy formulation and implementation came together, in the making of funding decisions. Significant, too, is that on the microboard model the bureaucracy engages in sanctioned advocacy on behalf of the individual and those in the individual's circle of support. Responsibility and accountability for funding rest with the individual, his or her microboard, and a representative of the bureaucracy whose advocacy is legitimated. This increases the chances of there being continuity of support and thus greater coherence in the person's life. The presence of both paid and unpaid support provides for renewal of energy among microboard members.

The state has a key role to play if our goal is to achieve empowerment-in-community. In successful microboards, government facilitators are key partners.

Unlike most traditional case managers, the role of these facilitators has been conceived in a way to make explicit their mandate to contribute towards enhancing texture. They do not make decisions, but instead provide information and suggest options to the microboard based on what they know about the individual's goals and dreams. Instead of forming partnerships with transfer agencies, facilitators work directly in partnership with the individual with a disability. The facilitator is not a mere representative of a large, service delivery system, but a partner in an open, community-based network, where the interests of the individual and the collective tend to become one.

In writing this book, we have tried to reflect what people told us about their individual life situations, and how they felt about their life experiences. Our hope is that we have been true to the meaning of their stories and that the voices we heard—of the many individuals with disabilities, family members, friends, and support staff that we met across the country—have been fairly represented here. Of the various approaches to support that we observed, individualized funding *along with* a microboard service model seemed most promising in terms of fostering empowerment-in-community and the realization of texture in people's lives. We doubt that either one of these approaches, individualized funding or the microboard, would function particularly well without the other. We saw instances where people were receiving individualized funding, but their supports remained outside a microboard structure. They received services from agencies, many of which operated within the private, for-profit sector. It appeared that individualized funding in privatized, for-profit services functioned less satisfactorily when measured against the standard of empowerment-in-community than it did when it was embedded in the microboard model. Under the private, for-profit approach, people remained somewhat isolated, contained in a world of disability for the most part, leading lives that were fragmented into privatized service compartments. Privatized, for-profit services to vulnerable citizens create a system which has little protection against carelessness and neglect. Telling in this regard was that none among the 112 private, for-profit agencies that responded to our survey noted advocacy as part of its mandate.

Increasingly, different regions of Canada are examining alternatives to program funding. Funding individuals with developmental disabilities rather than funding programs is at least an idea that is now being taken more seriously. Indirect individualized funding, where funds continue to be transferred to agencies but are individualized, in relation to an estimate of the cost of care and support of each person who receives service from any particular agency, is one alternative that is being considered. It holds promise in terms of regarding the person as central to the provision of those supports that enable him or her to live, work and enjoy a rich life in the community. As well, indirect individualized funding may respond to the need for reassurance that communities will maintain the vast pool of knowledge and expertise that currently exists within community agencies. But indirect individualized funding channelled to an agency that has the task of efficiently serving large numbers of people is not likely to encourage mutuality and, despite good intentions, is likely to depersonalize its "clients." Similarly, this approach to support may not bring clarity to the question of accountability of those around the person. Under the microboard model, by contrast, there is no such ambiguity—accountability is to the person at the centre of the circle of support.

Turning Promising Ideas into Practice

If a genuinely empowering philosophy of practice, directed toward empowerment-in-community, were fully embraced by policy makers, traditional service agencies would be radically transformed. In fact, one might wonder whether the traditional service agencies would have any role to play if the empowerment paradigm were to be universally employed and fully realized in practice. Rioux et al. (1997) argue, however, that within less traditional approaches to support, there may well be an important role for organized support agencies, such as ensuring access to services in geographically remote locations, providing ongoing support to families, and carrying out education and collective advocacy. In any case, any change is likely to happen slowly, and traditional agencies have a wealth of knowledge and skill that cannot be assumed to be obsolete under new paradigms of support. What this suggests though, is another question. How can agencies alter their practices in order to provide support in ways which enhance texture and foster empowerment-in-community?

An important first step would be to give people with disabilities and their families a role in the hiring, placement, and supervision of staff members and, beyond this, a role in the process of making decisions of all kinds. While people's input into decisions about their services has certainly increased in recent years, participatory approaches to agency management have been less common. Fostering textured lives means seeing the needs and capacities of individuals in a social ecological context. Boards and committees of agencies need connection to the real life experiences of the people they serve in order to guide their agencies towards a new philosophy of practice. For this is to happen, it seems clear that government must not only increase, but also rethink, its role in the system.

What recommendations do these reflections suggest? We are led to the idea of a model based on the person-centred principles that underlie microboards. The principles are that the system of support should foster texture in the person's life, open pathways to the wider community, and be based on mutuality. If these principles are to be taken seriously, it is important that the system of support does not cast the person receiving support in the role of a dependent, that it be responsive to the person's individual needs and preferences, and that it does not enclose the person in a subworld of disability. Possibly a model system of support based on microboard principles would not incorporate all of the features of the microboards that currently exist. Also, there might well be situations where the microboard approach is not feasible. For example, there may be no one available to serve on the microboard. Nevertheless, because microboards are far and away the best current exemplars of the two principles on which we believe the system of support for developmentally disabled adults should be founded, it seems appropriate to call the system we are describing here the microboard model.

Under the new model, microboards might be thought of as small collectives, forming hubs to which society delegates its collective responsibility to persons with disabilities. These hubs would coexist with and complement community agencies which deliver direct services as needed and appropriate. The objective would be to open the wider community to people with disabilities and to eliminate their dependency on the traditional community agencies. To accomplish these objectives, people with disabilities and their microboards would be entrusted with sufficient funds to enable them to meet their needs. Community agencies would continue to receive core funding. To meet some of their needs, the individuals and their microboards would likely want to purchase services from these agencies. But because they had financial resources of their own, they would be able to "shop around," with the result that the traditional agencies would need to become more responsive to the preferences of those they serve. These arrangements would go some distance toward eliminating dependency. As well, openness to the community would be enhanced: with the funds at their disposal, individuals with a disability would be able to meet the extra costs often incurred—for instance, those for transportation and equipment—when they wish to access mainstream services already in place for the community at large, such as public pools, ice rinks, schools, libraries, hospitals, shopping centres, and recreation centres.

It would be absolutely essential that individualized funding be kept at an adequate level. Shifting a portion of the funding from the agencies to individuals should not be an occasion for reducing *overall* funding, as was often the case during the deinstitutionalization period, when the return to the community was not accompanied by provision of adequate services for individuals in the community. The microboard approach to support is in many ways similar to certain other individualized approaches that we have seen emerge over the past decade, such as circles of support, wraparound, and support clusters. What distinguishes the microboard approach from these other individualized approaches to support is that the individual, through the microboard structure, receives and controls the dollars with which to hire staff and to purchase services and resources as he or she chooses.

Broader and wider reliance on the microboard model would respond to the principal problem we have identified with the present system. It would redress the power imbalance that currently exists between the agencies and individuals with developmental disabilities. This imbalance underlies the state of dependency into which the system thrusts these individuals. An obvious question, of course, is whether a microboard could become insensitive to the needs and perspective of the person with a disability at its centre. If this were to happen, however, it would indicate a breakdown in the microboard-based system, a local failure. By contrast, under the present system, dominated by program funding and agency control, dependency is not a sign of breakdown; it is designed into the system. It is easier to correct a failure in a system designed to *overcome* dependency, than it is to keep a system designed to *induce* dependency from actually having that result.

The people we met in microboards all had very complex disabilities, more so than the individuals we met who lived under other models of support. They were all non-verbal and non-ambulatory and they all had high medical needs. With that goes, of course, a high degree of physical dependence, which in itself sets them apart from most of the other study participants. However, if people with complex disabilities can be supported in ways that allow their strengths and capacities to emerge and their lives to gain texture, then surely for those with less complex needs the microboard model of support would yield equally significant results.

To date, direct individualized funding has been an option only for those who are deemed impossible to serve within traditional models. What we have found is that people who appear least likely to be able to pursue independent lives when seen through a traditional "quality of service" lens are, in practice, living more textured lives than their putatively less disabled peers. The microboard model is unique and innovative because it forces state representatives into new and more constructive roles, because it vests control with individuals and families, and because it is grounded in openness to the larger community.

Another approach to providing direct individualized funding involves designating a public trustee who in some ways takes the place of the microboard. The trustee's role is to authorize expenditures of the funds that have been directed to the person with a disability. One potential problem with this approach is that the trustee may exercise his or her responsibilities in a way that is insensitive to the needs of the person being supported, either by imposing a view regarding how the funds should be used or at least by insisting on authorizing each and every expenditure, small as well as large. On the other hand, if the trustee does not err in these ways, there is a danger that the individual will be left without the necessary care and support, isolated from the wider community. In this case, the trustee approach is susceptible to the criticism that it does nothing more than privatize and commercialize support, in that it establishes the person being supported as a consumer, shopping around for needed services.

In any event, the trustee version of direct individualized funding is a funding arrangement and nothing more, a way of channelling support funds to the person with a disability and of ensuring accountability to the funder. By contrast, the microboard approach is much more than a funding arrangement and is concerned with much more than how support funds are channelled to the person with a disability and how these funds are spent. The microboard provides a circle of support that both forms a microcommunity for the person with a disability and opens the desired pathways to the community at large. In these ways, it works for empowerment-in-community.

Empowerment-in-Community as the Preeminent Public Good

In chapter 1 we introduced the idea of empowerment-in-community and suggested that, although it expressed a fundamental value that motivated us to undertake this study, in the context of our research it had the status of a sensitizing idea. It was to alert us to possibilities, but not form a grid that dictated an interpretation we were committed to in advance. The more we spoke with people with developmental disabilities and those in their circles of support, however, the more confident we became that our sensitizing idea captured fairly well the values and motivational orientation of those with whom we were speaking. This is not to say, of course, that the term "empowerment-in-community" ever surfaced in those conversations. But it was clear that the people with whom we spoke were oriented toward the very issues that one who values empowerment-in-community must regard as most significant: Is one finding ways to engage in the life of the wider community—by getting a job that pays a decent wage, travelling to a distant place, securing a home of one's own, making friends? Where individuals did not aspire to these everyday aspects of normal life, thinking it unrealistic to hope for so much, they typically conveyed a sense of missing something important. The resultant lack of texture in their lives was felt by them and not merely attributed to their situation by us.

How could it be otherwise? A good job, travel, a home, friends. These matter to everyone. But why do they matter? It seemed clear that they matter to adults with developmental disabilities for the same reasons that they matter to the rest of us. We may use different language to say it. Of a good job, apart from expressing our interest in having a decent wage, we may say that we like the challenge, that we want to be doing something worthwhile, that we want to be helping other people, that the work is just intrinsically interesting to us. Of travel, we may say that it widens our horizons, satisfies our curiosity, brings us into contact with others who are different from us. Of having a home of our own, we may say that it gives us somewhere to bring our friends, a secure place in the community, roots. Of friends, we may say that it gets us out of ourselves, satisfies our desire to share ourselves and our lives with others.

It is notable that answers such as these fall into two groups. Some express the idea that one thinks that a good job, travel, a home, and friends will contribute to personal growth and development—that they will be empowering. Others express the related idea, that through these activities and relationships one will connect with others in relationships of community and find meaning in that connection. But it is the same activities and relationships that are found to be both empowering and sources of belonging to a community. So, we all, at this level, those of us who are not labelled and those of us who are, see no opposition between empowerment and community, but instead confidently believe that they are found in tandem. What we seek is empowerment-in-community.

In the end, the weakness of the traditional support system, with its network of specially designed programs for "the disabled," is that it works against empowerment-in-community and thus washes out the texture in people's lives. The strength of the microboard approach to support of adults with developmental disabilities is that it is inspired by the values that "empowerment-in-community" encapsulates.

Empowerment-in-community, and its realization in textured lives, is not merely a value for those who are disabled. It is a condition that we all seek. As such, it is the preeminent public good. Thus, policies that work toward empowerment-in-community are in everyone's interest. If we find the will to adopt the microboard approach to support in all of our communities, so that a nearly invisible and highly marginalized segment of the community may begin to be and be seen as being part of the mainstream, we will all be better off. We will no longer need to blind ourselves to the presence amongst us of fellow citizens who are shut out from what is for us normal life. More important, perhaps, we will all be empowered by the widening and strengthening of our communities that results from an openness that includes everyone.

APPENDIX I

The Research Project: Survey Data

There were several stages to this study of the life experiences of adults with developmental disabilities in Canada. First, to establish a detailed picture of the service landscape as this affects adults with developmental disabilities, we surveyed 1336 agencies in Canada that supported adults with developmental disabilities.[1] Responses were received from 801 agencies that provided support services to a total of 63,188 adults with developmental disabilities.[2]

The survey asked questions regarding the number of people served, the range of services provided, funding procedures, planning of services and supports, whether families were involved in the lives of the individuals served, and whether the agency had participation from community members, family members, and persons with disabilities on their boards and committees. The result offered a very extensive picture of support services for adults with developmental disabilities living in Canada. A summary of these data follows in tables AI-1 to AI-7.

Table AI-1 sets out the size of the groups served by agencies in each province. This shows how large or small the groupings of people were generally within agencies across the country. It appears that the agencies serving a smaller number of people generally operated in western and eastern Canada, especially in British Columbia, while the larger agencies are in the central part of the country.

---

[1] These were agencies that we were able to reach via provincial government ministries responsible for funding services to adults with developmental disabilities. We also obtained membership listings from all provincial Associations for Community Living, so that our survey population included all service providers that were members of provincial Associations for Community Living, as well as those agencies that were receiving government funding from their respective provinces. The primary criterion for inclusion in the survey was the receipt of government funding for at least part of their day-to-day operations.

[2] The total number supported may include people served by more than one agency, i.e., there may be double counting of people who, for instance, have been counted by a residential service provider in a particular community, and counted again by a separate agency which provides some of those same people with another service, such as vocational or life skills training.

For instance, approximately 65% of the British Columbia agencies we heard from served 1 to 10 people, and approximately 34% of the agencies in Ontario served more than 100 people. In Quebec, 2% of the agencies provided services to 10 or fewer individuals, while more than half (55.5%) provided services to groups of 100 or more. In other provinces the majority of the agencies provided services to groups of more moderate sizes.

Table AI-1
Number of Agencies by Province, Grouped According to Number of Adults Served (% in prov.)

No. of Adults Served	NWT/ YK	BC	AB	SK	MB	ON	PQ	NB	NS	PE	NF	Total
1-10	1 (16.7)	126 (64.6)	13 (13.7)	13 (21.3)	17 (29.8)	10 (4.4)	1 (2.0)	6 (11.3)	7 (33.3)	2 (13.3)	4 (19.0)	200
11-20	1 (16.7)	15 (7.7)	13 (13.7)	10 (16.4)	10 (17.5)	19 (8.3)	4 (8.2)	13 (24.5)	5 (23.8)	3 (20.0)	2 (9.5)	95
21-50	2 (33.3)	21 (10.8)	29 (30.5)	16 (26.2)	14 (24.6)	50 (21.9)	7 (14.3)	21 (39.6)	5 (23.8)	4 (26.7)	9 (42.9)	178
51-100	1 (16.7)	8 (4.1)	21 (22.1)	2 (3.3)	9 (15.8)	47 (20.6)	3 (6.1)	3 (5.7)	3 (14.3)	3 (20.0)	2 (9.5)	102
> 100	0 (0)	11 (5.6)	15 (15.8)	11 (18.0)	5 (8.8)	77 (33.8)	27 (55.1)	4 (7.5)	1 (4.8)	2 (13.3)	1 (4.8)	154
not known	1 (16.7)	14 (7.2)	4 (4.2)	9 (14.8)	2 (3.5)	25 (11.0)	7 (14.3)	6 (11.3)	0 (0)	1 (6.7)	3 (14.3)	72
Total	6	195	95	61	57	228	49	53	21	15	21	801

In order to explore funding arrangements, the survey took into account a range of funding possibilities. Respondents were provided with the following operational definitions (see chart AI-1) for each funding category and asked to indicate whether they did or did not utilize each funding approach. Accordingly, agencies that operated with more than one form of funding could report that.

Chart AI-1
Funding Definitions

Funding Approach:	Operational definition:
• Program funding	Transfer agency funded for different programs offered; for example, vocational, residential, recreational, etc., with no funds allocated to individuals.
• Global funding	Transfer or other agency allocated funds from program funding to support each individual according to his or her needs.
• Indirect individual funding	Transfer agency received funds on behalf of the individual for his or her specific supports or services.
• Direct individual funding	Funds transferred to the control of the individual and or family, with the individual and or family purchasing services from the transfer agency or from other service providers, as they so chose.

Across the country program funding continued to dominate. However, in table AI-2 we see some clear differences across the country in relation to individualized funding approaches. The majority of the *direct* individualized funding was taking place in the west (British Columbia and Alberta). Alberta had most clearly pursued policies geared to individualized funding with 66% of the agency activity in the province utilizing direct individualized funding. It is interesting to note, particularly in Manitoba and Nova Scotia, that a fair percentage of agencies were involved in serving people with *indirect* individual funding.

Table AI-2
Number of Agencies Using Various Funding Approaches in Each Province (% in prov.)

Funding Approach	NWT/ YK	BC	AB	SK	MB	ON	PQ	NB	NS	PE	NF	Total
Program	6 (100.0)	93 (47.7)	72 (75.8)	48 (78.7)	38 (66.7)	200 (87.7)	17 (34.7)	27 (50.9)	8 (38.1)	14 (93.3)	13 (61.9)	536
Indirect individual	0 (0)	60 (30.8)	33 (34.7)	17 (27.9)	27 (47.4)	75 (32.9)	6 (12.2)	12 (22.6)	11 (52.4)	3 (20.0)	9 (42.9)	253
Global	0 (0)	41 (21.0)	11 (11.6)	10 (16.4)	9 (15.8)	48 (21.1)	17 (34.7)	14 (26.4)	4 (19.0)	4 (26.7)	9 (42.9)	167
Direct individual	0 (0)	43 (22.1)	63 (66.3)	7 (11.5)	7 (12.3)	22 (9.6)	6 (12.2)	6 (11.3)	0 (0)	1 (6.7)	0 (0)	155

Note: Some agencies use more than one funding approach; therefore total column percentages exceed 100.

In part, as a response to the demands of advocates and self-advocates, the planning of services and support has become more participatory and inclusive of individuals with developmental disabilities and of their families. Table AI-3 indicates that the main planning approach used across Canada was team planning, which meant that in most instances agencies tried to involve staff, family members, and the individuals themselves in the planning process. The shift toward planning controlled by the individual was seen most prominently in British Columbia, Alberta, and Ontario, where survey respondents indicated a fair percentage of service planning was determined by the individuals they supported.

Table AI-3
Number of Agencies Using Various Planning Approaches in Each Province (% in prov.)

Planning Approach	NWT/ YK	BC	AB	SK	MB	ON	PQ	NB	NS	PE	NF	Total
By team	5 (83.3)	147 (75.4)	73 (76.8)	51 (83.6)	54 (94.7)	192 (84.2)	28 (57.1)	37 (69.8)	18 (85.7)	14 (93.3)	17 (81.0)	**636**
By individual	1 (16.7)	74 (37.9)	34 (35.8)	6 (9.8)	14 (24.6)	119 (52.2)	14 (28.6)	8 (15.1)	4 (19.0)	2 (13.3)	6 (28.6)	**282**
By agency	2 (33.3)	49 (25.1)	12 (12.6)	11 (18.0)	12 (21.1)	37 (16.2)	14 (28.6)	18 (34.0)	4 (19.0)	4 (26.7)	8 (38.1)	**171**

Note: Some agencies use more than one planning approach; therefore total column percentages exceed 100.

Table AI-4 summarizes the residential services offered by survey respondents. Across all provinces group homes continue to dominate the living arrangements for adults with developmental disabilities. However, a fair percentage of agencies are supporting people in apartment living. Other residential services also figure fairly high and cover a range of housing arrangements, including proprietary homes (one to two people in someone's home), persons living in a family setting, or in their own home with the support of a microboard, adoptive families, respite care (where a service provider offers a bed on a temporary basis to relieve the primary caregiver), transitional housing, and institutional settings (e.g., training centres, behaviour management centres, regional centres, and retirement homes).

Table AI-4
Number of Agencies Providing Residential Services within Each Province (% in prov.)

Residential Services	NWT/ YK	BC	AB	SK	MB	ON	PQ	NB	NS	PE	NF	Total
Group homes	2 (33.3)	59 (30.3)	42 (44.2)	33 (54.1)	34 (59.7)	122 (53.5)	20 (40.8)	17 (32.1)	13 (61.9)	8 (53.3)	6 (28.6)	356
Supported apartments	1 (16.7)	31 (15.9)	34 (35.8)	18 (29.5)	22 (38.6)	121 (53.1)	15 (30.6)	12 (22.6)	5 (23.8)	6 (40.0)	4 (19.1)	269
Other residential	3 (50.0)	51 (26.2)	26 (27.4)	10 (16.4)	9 (15.8)	62 (27.2)	14 (28.6)	2 (3.8)	8 (38.1)	4 (26.7)	1 (4.8)	190
Foster family	2 (33.3)	34 (17.4)	15 (15.8)	1 (1.6)	6 (10.5)	47 (20.6)	17 (34.7)	6 (11.3)	3 (14.3)	5 (33.3)	2 (9.5)	138
Natural parents	0 (0)	18 (9.2)	25 (26.3)	9 (14.8)	7 (12.3)	44 (19.3)	14 (28.6)	5 (9.4)	0 (0)	4 (26.7)	4 (19.1)	130
Homes with staff	0 (0)	23 (11.8)	6 (6.3)	7 (11.5)	11 (19.3)	9 (4.0)	6 (12.2)	3 (5.7)	1 (4.8)	2 (13.3)	6 (28.6)	74
Boarding homes	0 (0)	7 (3.6)	4 (4.2)	4 (6.6)	0 (0)	10 (4.4)	5 (10.2)	1 (1.9)	0 (0)	4 (26.7)	1 (4.8)	36

Note: Some agencies have several residential programs and so will appear more than once in these data. Therefore, total column percentages exceed 100.

In vocational services, people are engaged in a variety of pursuits, ranging from training centres to supported employment and small businesses, as outlined in table AI-5. In general, most people are congregated in life skills and sheltered workshop or training centre programs. Supported employment programs exist in most areas, although often people will spend only part of their day or week in supported employment, returning to the sheltered workshop for the balance of the working week. Training centres figured significantly lower in the Northwest Territories/Yukon, British Columbia, Alberta, Quebec, and Newfoundland (less than 25% of the agencies in each of these provinces and territories). In the provinces of Saskatchewan, Manitoba, Ontario, New Brunswick, Nova Scotia, and Prince Edward Island, training centres were reported by a high proportion of agencies (greater than 33% of the agencies in each province). Included in the other vocational category were volunteer work, farming, contract jobs, transportation and prevocational training, retirement programs, and recreational or social pursuits. These figured highly in Alberta and Ontario.

Table AI-5
Number of Agencies Offering Vocational Services in Each Province (% in prov.)

Vocational Services	NWT/ YK	BC	AB	SK	MB	ON	PQ	NB	NS	PE	NF	Total
Life skills	3 (50.0)	74 (38.0)	42 (44.2)	21 (34.4)	19 (33.3)	108 (47.4)	16 (32.7)	26 (49.1)	6 (28.6)	6 (40.0)	6 (28.6)	327
Supported employment	3 (50.0)	47 (24.1)	48 (40.5)	22 (36.1)	27 (47.4)	107 (46.9)	18 (36.7)	26 (49.1)	6 (28.6)	9 (60.0)	12 (57.1)	325
Sheltered workshop	1 (16.7)	27 (13.9)	23 (24.2)	26 (42.6)	27 (47.4)	83 (36.4)	10 (20.4)	22 (41.5)	7 (33.3)	9 (60.0)	5 (23.8)	240
Other vocational	1 (16.7)	37 (19.0)	40 (42.1)	8 (13.1)	13 (22.8)	69 (30.3)	7 (14.3)	2 (3.8)	0 (0)	2 (13.3)	2 (9.5)	181

Note: Some agencies offer more than one vocational service and will appear more than once in these data. Therefore, total column percentages exceed 100.

Across all provinces, agencies provided a variety of other services (see table AI-6). Advocacy, recreation/social/travel, and community education were the three main service areas provided outside of residential and vocational services, with more than half of the agencies in each province engaging in these forms of service delivery. Consumer education, monitoring services, information resources, respite, and self-help were among the services offered. Included in the category of other supports were therapy and counselling, assessment, case management, friendship circles and circles of support, special services at home, drop-in centres, parent or caregiver support, and trusteeships. Service brokerage figured less prominently, with the highest proportions reported in the provinces of Alberta and Ontario. It is important to note that while some provinces have a very large number of "other" support services, in fact agencies may be funded to provide a range of programs, so that these figures represent all of the programs or services offered by the agencies from whom we heard. This means, then, that many agencies—especially some of the larger traditional transfer agencies in Ontario and Quebec that serve over one hundred people—having something of a monopoly over the services that are available, may provide a very large range of these other support services,. Again, total column percentages will exceed one hundred because they reflect the proportion each activity or service represents of the total services available in each province.

Table AI-6
Number of Agencies Providing Other Support Services in Each Province (% in prov.)

Other Services	NWT/ YK	BC	AB	SK	MB	ON	PQ	NB	NS	PE	NF	Total
Advocacy	6 (100)	132 (67.7)	80 (84.2)	38 (62.3)	38 (66.7)	195 (85.5)	43 (87.8)	38 (71.7)	15 (71.4)	12 (80.0)	16 (76.2)	613
Rec./ social/ travel	5 (83.3)	136 (69.7)	71 (74.7)	49 (80.3)	43 (75.4)	169 (74.1)	41 (83.7)	36 (67.9)	16 (76.2)	12 (80.0)	10 (47.6)	588
Community education	5 (83.3)	101 (51.8)	73 (76.8)	34 (55.7)	32 (56.1)	186 (81.6)	13 (26.5)	32 (60.4)	16 (76.2)	10 (66.7)	12 (57.1)	514
Consumer education	2 (33.3)	101 (51.8)	66 (69.5)	25 (41.0)	28 (49.1)	174 (76.3)	35 (71.4)	29 (54.7)	12 (57.1)	9 (60.0)	11 (52.4)	492
Monitoring services	4 (66.7)	77 (39.5)	55 (57.9)	35 (57.4)	24 (42.1)	131 (57.5)	25 (51.0)	34 (64.2)	11 (52.4)	8 (53.3)	12 (57.1)	416
Information resource	4 (66.7)	50 (25.6)	45 (47.4)	18 (29.5)	12 (21.1)	119 (52.2)	31 (63.3)	12 (22.6)	8 (38.1)	5 (33.3)	7 (33.3)	311
Respite	1 (13.7)	67 (34.4)	38 (40.0)	19 (31.1)	21 (36.8)	113 (49.6)	9 (18.4)	16 (30.2)	10 (47.6)	10 (66.7)	4 (19.1)	308
Self-help groups	2 (33.3)	56 (28.7)	42 (44.2)	17 (27.9)	7 (12.3)	112 (49.1)	25 (51.0)	19 (35.9)	9 (42.9)	3 (20.0)	9 (42.9)	301
Other supports	1 (16.7)	36 (18.5)	28 (29.5)	7 (11.5)	10 (17.5)	72 (31.6)	3 (6.1)	13 (24.5)	4 (19.1)	3 (20.0)	3 (14.3)	180
Service brokerage	0 (0)	17 (8.7)	27 (28.4)	6 (9.8)	7 (12.3)	69 (30.3)	8 (16.3)	3 (5.7)	4 (19.1)	1 (6.7)	4 (19.1)	146

Participating agencies were asked to outline their mandate or mission statement. A total of 737 respondents did this. These statements were content analyzed using a textual coding scheme. The conceptual framework used for the content analysis was based on the four major philosophies of service detailed in chapter 2, i.e., advocacy, normalization/social role valorization (SRV), quality service, and capacity building, with latent coding being used to capture meanings which were embedded in the mission statement texts. The coding scheme used in this analysis is summarized below in chart 2.

Chart 2

Latent Coding Scheme

If the text included any of the following key words:	Coded as:
• Advocate on behalf of • Speak out for the rights of • Gain access to services for	Advocacy
• Live as normal a life as possible • Integrate into the community • Live as valued member of their community	Normalization/SRV
• Manage safe and efficient services • Administer good services • Provide support services	"Quality" Service
• Identify people's capabilities and strengths • Help people live independently • Live active lives as contributing members of society	Capacity Building

As discussed in chapter 2, the dominant philosophy among these 737 survey respondents was "quality" service. Some evidence of the more progressive values associated with capacity building existed, while relatively few agencies incorporated normalization/social role valorization, or advocacy in their mission statements (see table AI-7).

Table AI-7
Service Philosophies Reflected in Mission Statements or Mandates

Philosophy	Percentage of survey respondents
"Quality" Service	55%
Capacity Building	28%
Normalization/Social Role Valorization	11%
Advocacy	6%

APPENDIX II

The Qualitative Interview Participants

Agency Type	Adults	Family Members	Staff	Management	Owner
Private, non-profit **75% PF**	Claude		1		
	Ryan		1		
	Michelle		1		
	Marie		1		
	Hubert		1		
				1	
Totals	5		5	1	
Microboards **(4)** **100% DIF**	Josephine*	mother	1		
	Colin *	mother & father	2		
	Richard *	mother			
	Kate *		1	1***	
Totals	4	4	4	1***	
Private, for-profit **100% DIF**	Ron **		2		
	Bev **	mother	1		
	Bonnie **	mother	1		
	Chad **	mother	1		
	Nick		1		
	Joan *		1		
	Joe	mother			
	Margaret		1		
	Mary **	sister	1		
	Paul **	brother	1		
			4		1****
Totals	10	6	14		1****

Agency Type	Adults	Family Members	Staff	Management	Owner
Private, for-profit **100% IIF** **20% GF**	Barbara | Christine | Elizabeth** John ** George ** Mary Ellen**	mother	1 1 1 1 1 1 3		1****
Totals	6	1	8		1****
Public, non-profit **100% IIF**	Lorraine Françoise Jean Ricardo Joyce		1 1 1 1 1	1	
Totals	5		5	1	
Public, non-profit **90% PF** **10% IIF**	Chris Lori ** | Judy | Jack Esther Howard ** Norma | Jane ** | Sarah ** Steve Keith ** Roger *	2 sisters mother father	1 1 1 1 1 1 1 1 1 4	1	
Totals	12	4	13	1	

Agency Type	Adults	Family Members	Staff	Management	Owner
Public, non-profit 100% PF	Harry	mother			
	Beatrice **	mother	1		
	Belinda *	mother	1		
	Betsy **	mother & father	1		
	Geraldine **	sister	1		
	Dilon **	mother	1		
	Eileen *	mother	1		
	Julie	brother			
	Tanya *	mother	1		
	Ann **	mother			
				1	
Totals	10	11	7	1	

Legend

*	Non-verbal, support present in interview	PF	Program funding
**	Support present in interview	GF	Global funding
***	Microboard member	IIF	Indirect individualized funding
****	Owner operator	DIF	Direct individualized funding

REFERENCES

Agosta, J. (1989). Using cash assistance to support family efforts. In G. Singer & L. Irvin (Eds.), *Support for caregiving families: Enabling positive adaptation to disability* (pp. 189-204). Baltimore, MD: Paul H. Brookes.

Armitage, A. (1996). *Social welfare in Canada revisited: Facing up to the future*. Don Mills, ON: Oxford University Press.

Ashbaugh, J., & Smith, G. (1996). Beware the managed health-care companies. *Mental Retardation, 34*(3) 189-193.

Bercovici, S.M. (1983). *Barriers to normalization: The restrictive management of retarded persons.* Baltimore, MD: University Park Press.

Bogdan, R., & Taylor, S. J. (1994). *The social meaning of mental retardation: Two life stories.* New York: Teachers College Press.

Borthwick-Duffy, S.A. (1996). Evaluation and measurement of quality of life: Special considerations for persons with mental retardation. In R.L. Schalock (Ed.), *Quality of life, Vol.1: Conceptualization and measurement* (pp.105-119). Washington, DC: AAMR.

Botschner, J.V. (1996). Reconsidering male friendships: A social-development perspective. In C. Tolman, F. Cherry, R. van Hezewijk & I. Lubek (Eds.), *Problems of theoretical psychology* (pp. 242-253). Toronto: Captus Press.

Bradley, V.J. (1994). Evolution of a new service paradigm. In V.J. Bradley, J.W. Ashbaugh, & B.C. Blaney (Eds.), *Creating individual supports for people with developmental disabilities: A mandate for change at many levels* (pp. 2-32). Baltimore, MD: Paul H. Brookes.

Bradley, V.J., Ashbaugh, & Blaney, B.C. (Eds.). (1994). *Creating individual supports for people with developmental disabilities: A mandate for change at many levels* (pp. 2-32). Baltimore, MD: Paul H. Brookes.

Canadian Association for Community Living. (1998). *Overcoming disability as a socioeconomic condition: An international paradigm shift.* North York, ON: Roeher Institute.

Carling, P. (1995). *Return to community: Building support systems for people with psychiatric disabilities.* New York: The Guilford Press.

Carniol, B. (1995). *Case critical: Challenging social services in Canada.* (3rd ed.) Toronto: Between the Lines.

Centre for Research and Education in Human Services. (1988). *Independence and control: Today's dream, tomorrow's reality.* Kitchener, ON: Author.

Centre for Research and Education in Human Services. (1993). *Review of individualized funding.* Kitchener, ON: Author.

Christenson, J.A., Fendley, K., & Robinson, J.W. (1989). In J.A. Christenson & J.R. Robinson (Eds.) *Community development in perspective* (pp. 3-25). Ames, IA: Iowa State University Press.

Djao, A.W. (1983). *Inequality and social policy: The sociology of welfare.* Toronto: John Wiley & Sons.

Dowson, S. (1991). *Moving to the dance or service culture and community care.* London: Values into Action.

Dunst, C.J., Trivette, C.M., & Lapointe, N. (1992). Toward clarification of the meaning and the key elements of empowerment. *Family Science Review, 5*(1 & 2), 111-130.

Dunst, C.J., Trivette, C.M., Starnes, A.L., Hamby, D.W., & Gordon, N.J. (1993). *Building and evaluating family support initiatives: A national study of programs for persons with developmental disabilities.* Baltimore, MD: Paul H. Brookes Publishing Co.

Dybwad, R. (1990). *Perspectives on a parent movement: The revolt of parents of children with intellectual limitations.* Cambridge, MA: Brookline Books.

Florin, P., & Wandersman, A. (1990). An introduction to citizen participation, voluntary organizations, and community development: Insights for empowerment through research. *American Journal of Community Psychology, 18*(1), 41-54.

Forsey, H. (1993). *Circles of strength: community alternatives to alienation.* Gabriola Island, BC: New Society Publishers.

Friedman, J. (1992). *Empowerment: The politics of alternative development.* Cambridge, MA: Blackwell Publishers.

Glaser, B.G., & Strauss, A.L. (1967). *The discovery of grounded theory.* New York: Aldine.

Gottlieb, B. (1985). Social networks and social support: An overview of research, practice and policy implications. *Health Education Quarterly, 12*(1), 5-22.

Gottlieb, B. (1998). Support groups. In H. S. Friedman. *Encyclopedia of mental health.* San Francisco, CA: Academic Press.

Guest, D. (1985). *The emergence of social security in Canada.* Vancouver, BC: University of British Columbia Press.

Handler, J.F. (1986). *The conditions of discretion: Autonomy, community, bureaucracy.* New York: Russell Sage Foundation.

Haworth, L. (1977). *Decadence and objectivity.* Toronto: University of Toronto Press.

Haworth, L. (1986). *Autonomy.* New Haven, CN: Yale University Press.

Hayden, M.F., & Abery, B.H. (Eds.). (1994). *Challenges for a service system in transition: Ensuring quality community experiences for persons with developmental disabilities.* Baltimore, MD: Paul H. Brookes Publishing Co.

Hughes, C., & Hwang, B. (1996). Attempts to conceptualize and measure quality of life. In R.L. Schalock (Ed.), *Quality of life, Vol.1: Conceptualization and measurement* (pp. 51-62). Washington, DC: AAMR.

Hutchison, P., & McGill, J. (1998). *Community, integration, and leisure.* Toronto: Leisurability Publications.

Jones, T.M., Garlow, J.A., Turnbull, H.R., III, & Barber, P.A. (1996). Family empowerment in a family support program. In G.H.S. Singer, L.E. Powers, & A.L. Olson (Eds.), *Redefining family support: Innovations in public-private partnerships* (pp. 87-112). Baltimore, MD: Paul H. Brookes Publishing Co.

Jongbloed, L., & Crichton, A. (1990). Difficulties in shifting from individualistic to socio-political policy regarding disability in Canada. *Disability, Handicap and Society, 5,* 25-35.

Kirby, S., & McKenna, K. (1989). *Experience, research, social change: Methods from the margins.* Toronto: Garamond Press.

Kretzman, J., & McKnight, J. (1993). *Building communities from the inside out: A path towards finding and mobilizing a community's assets.* Chicago, IL: ACTA Publications.

Kuyek, J., & Labonté, R. (1995). *From power-over to power-with: Transforming professional practice.* Saskatoon, SK: Prairie Region Health Promotion Research Centre.

Laing, W. (1991). *Empowering the elderly: Direct consumer funding of care services.* London: The Institute of Economic Affairs/IEA Health and Welfare Unit.

Lightman, E.S. (1986, March). The impact of government economic restraint on mental health services in Canada. *Canada's Mental Health*, 24-28.

Lord, J. (1991). *Lives in transition: The process of personal empowerment.* Kitchener, ON: Centre for Research and Education in Human Services.

Lord, J., & Hutchison, P. (1993). The process of empowerment: Implications for theory and practice. *Canadian Journal of Community Mental Health, 12*(1), 5-22.

Lord, J., & Hutchison, P. (1996). Living with a disability in Canada: Toward autonomy and integration. In The National Forum on Health, *Canada health action: Building on the legacy* (pp. 376-431). Ottawa: Les Editions MultiMondes.

Lord, J., & Pedlar, A. (1991). Life in the community: Four years after the closure of an institution. *Mental Retardation, 19*(4), 213-221.

Luckasson, R., & Spitalnik, D. (1994). Political and programmatic shifts of the 1992 AAMR definition of Mental Retardation. In V.J. Bradley, J.W. Ashbaugh, & B.C. Blaney (Eds.), *Creating individual supports for people with developmental disabilities: A mandate for change at many levels* (pp. 81-95). Baltimore, MD: Paul H. Brookes.

Marlett, N.J. (Ed.). (1988). *Independent service brokerage: Achieving consumer control through direct payment.* Calgary, AB: The Walter Dinsdale Centre.

McGilly, F. (1991). *An introduction to Canada's public social services.* Toronto: McClelland & Stewart.

McKnight, J. (1987). Regenerating community. *Social Policy, 17,* 54-58.

McKnight, J. (1995). *The careless society: Community and its counterfeits.* New York: Basic Books.

Meyer, L., Peck, C., & Brown, L. (Eds.). (1991). *Critical issues in the lives of people with severe disabilities.* Baltimore, MD: Paul H. Brookes.

Morris, J. (1997). Care or empowerment? A disability rights perspective. *Social Policy and Administration, 31*(1), 54-60.

Morse, J.M. (1997). Considering theory derived from qualitative research. In J.M. Morse (Ed.), *Completing a qualitative project: Details and dialogue* (pp.163-191). Thousand Oaks, CA: Sage Publications.

Moscovitch, A., & Albert, J. (Eds.). (1987). *The "benevolent" state: The growth of welfare in Canada.* Toronto: Garamond Press.

Mount, B. (1995). *Capacity works: Finding windows for change using personal futures planning.* New York: Graphic Futures.

Nirje, B. (1980). The normalization principle. In R.J. Flynn & K.E. Nitsch (Eds.), *Normalization, social integration and community services* (pp. 31-49). Baltimore, MD: University Park Press.

O'Brien, J., & O'Brien, C.L. (1991). *More than just a new address: Images of organizations for supported living agencies.* Lithonia, GA: Responsive Systems Associates.

Ochocka, J., Roth, D., Lord, J., & Macnaughton, E. (1993). *Support clusters project: Evaluation of a demonstration project.* Kitchener, ON: Centre for Research and Education in Human Services.

O'Connell, M. (1988). *The gift of hospitality: Opening the doors of community life to people with disabilities.* Evanston, IL: Northwestern University, Centre for Urban Affairs and Policy Research.

Ozer, E.M., & Bandura, A. (1990). Mechanisms governing empowerment effects: A self efficacy analysis. *Journal of Personality and Social Psychology, 58*(3), 472-86.

Parenti, M. (1978). *Power and the powerless.* New York: St. Martin's Press.

Peck, C.A. (1991). Linking values and science in social policy decisions affecting citizens with severe disabilities. In L. H. Meyer, C. A. Peck, & L. Brown (Eds.), *Critical issues in the lives of people with severe disabilities* (pp. 1-15). Baltimore, MD: Paul H. Brookes.

Pedlar, A. (1990). Normalization and integration: A look at the Swedish experience. *Mental Retardation, 28*(5), 275-282.

Pedlar, A. (1991). Supportive communities: The gap between ideology and social policy. *Environments, 21*(2), 1-7.

Putnam, R.D. (1996, Winter). The strange disappearance of civic America. *The American Prospect. 24*, 34-48.

Racino, J.A. (1992). Life in the community: The independent living and support paradigms. In F.R. Rusch, L. DeStefano, J. Chadsey-Rusch, L.A. Phelps, and D.E. Syzmanski (Eds.), *Transition from school to work for youth and adults with disabilities*. Sycamore, IL: Sycamore Publishing Co.

Racino, J.A. (1994). Creating change in states, agencies, and communities. In V.J. Bradley, J.W. Ashbaugh, & B.C. Blaney (Eds.), *Creating individual supports for people with developmental disabilities* (pp.171-196). Baltimore, MD: Paul H. Brookes Publishing Co.

Raphael, D., Brown, I., Renwick, R., & Rootman, I. (1996). *Quality of life: What are the implications for health promotion?* Toronto: Centre for Health Promotion.

Rioux, M., Bach, M., & Crawford, C. (1997). Citizenship and people with disabilities in Canada: Towards an elusive ideal. In P. Ramcharan, G. Roberts, G. Grant, & J. Borland (Eds.), *Empowerment in everyday life: Learning disability* (pp. 204-221). London: Jessica Kingsley Publishers.

Rioux, M., & Richler, D. (1995). Count us in: Lessons from Canada on strategies for social change. In T. Philpot & L. Ward (Eds.), *Values and visions: Changing ideas in services for people with learning difficulties* (pp. 377-388). Oxford: Butterworth Heinemann.

Roeher Institute. (1990). *Making friends: Developing relationships between people with disabilities and other members of the community*. North York, ON: Author.

Roeher Institute. (1991). *The power to choose*. North York, ON: Author.

Roeher Institute. (1993a). *Direct dollars*. North York, ON: Author.

Roeher Institute. (1993b). *Nothing personal: The need for personal supports in Canada*. North York, ON: Author.

Roeher Institute. (1993c). *Pathway to integration: Final report –Mainstream 1992*. Report to Ministers of Social Services on The Federal/Provincial/Territorial Review of Services Affecting Canadians with Disabilities. North York, ON: Author.

Roeher Institute. (1996). *Disability, community and society: Exploring the links*. North York, ON: Author.

Salisbury, B., Dickey, J., & Crawford, C. (1987). *Service brokerage: Individual empowerment and social service accountability.* North York, ON: Roeher Institute.

Saul, J. Ralston (1995). *The unconscious civilization.* Toronto: Anansi Press.

Schalock, R.L. (Ed.). (1997). *Quality of life, Vol II: Application to persons with disabilities.* Washington, DC: AAMR.

Serrano-Garcia, I. (1994). The ethics of the powerful and the power of ethics. *American Journal of Community Psychology, 22*(1), 1-20.

Shapiro, J. P. (1993). *No pity: People with disabilities forging a new civil rights movement.* New York: Random House.

Singer, G.H.S., & Powers, L.E. (1993). *Families, disability and empowerment: Active coping skills and strategies for family interventions.* Baltimore, MD: Paul H. Brookes Publishing Co.

Singer, J.C. (1993). *Group homes and community integration of developmentally disabled people: Micro-institutionalization?* London: Jessica Kingsley Publishers.

Taylor, S.J., Bogdan, R., & Lutfiyya, Z. (1995). (Eds.), *The variety of community experience.* Baltimore, MD: Paul H. Brookes Publishing Co.

Trainor, J., Pomeroy, E., & Pape, B. (1993). *A new framework for support for people with serious mental health problems.* Toronto: Canadian Mental Health Association.

VanDenberg, J.E., & Grealish, E.M. (1996). Individualized services and supports through the wraparound process: Philosophy and procedures. *Journal of Child and Family Studies*, 5(1), 1-15.

Wallerstein, N. (1993). Powerlessness, empowerment, and health: Implications for health promotion programs. *American Journal of Health Promotion, 6*(3), 197-205.

Wertheimer, A. (Ed.). (1995). *Circles of support: Building inclusive communities.* Mangotsfield, Bristol (UK): Circles Network UK.

Wharf, B. (1992). *Communities and social policy in Canada.* Toronto: McClelland & Stewart Inc.

Women's Research Centre (WRC) (1994). *Microboards review.* Vancouver, BC: Vela Housing Society.

Wolfensberger, W. (1983). Social role valorization: A proposed new term for the principle of normalization. *Mental Retardation, 21*(6), 234-39.

Wolfensberger, W. (1997). Major obstacles to rationality and quality of human services in contemporary society. In R. Adams (Ed.), *Crisis in the human services: National and international issues: Selected papers from a conference held at the University of Cambridge September 1996* (pp. 133-155). Kingston-upon-Hull, UK: University of Lincolnshire and Humberside.

Zimmerman, M.A., Israel, B.A., Schulz, A., & Checkoway, B. (1992). Further explorations in empowerment theory: An empirical analysis of psychological empowerment. *American Journal of Community Psychology, 20*(6), 707-727.

PARTICIPANT INDEX

SUBJECT INDEX

-D-

-E-

-F-

-J-

-K-

-L-

-M-

-N-

-O-

-S-